Manage
Your Critic

From Overwhelm to Clarity
in 7 Steps

A practical guide for parents,
managers and entrepreneurs

*You matter and
your story has
value.
Sheryl.*

Sheryl Andrews
The Strength and
Solution Detective

Contents

Acknowledgements

This has been one of the hardest parts of this book to write. I have been inspired, supported and challenged by so many different people at different times in my life. It feels impossible to narrow it down to a few lines. I am genuinely grateful to everyone, even those who unknowingly hurt me with their criticism – you made me who I am today.

My critic is also quick to remind me how I felt when my contribution was not acknowledged. With this in mind, if you read this acknowledgement and you have even the slightest twinge of "Why didn't she mention me?" then please pick up the phone and let's chat about that. It is not my intention to ignore or forget you and yet there are people in the past 12 months that have really stepped up and made a massive difference in my life and given me the support I needed to get this book finished, and there are some without whom this book would not have been possible.

David Grove – co-author with B.I. Panzer of *Resolving Traumatic Memories: Metaphors and Symbols in Psychotherapy* and originator of Clean Language, Clean Space and Emergent Knowledge – thank you for sharing your work on a generosity framework and providing me with access to the solution to my sensitivity to criticism.

Penny Tompkins and James Lawley – originators of Symbolic Modelling – thank you for making Clean Language accessible to so many.

Marian Way – author of *Clean Approaches for Coaches* – thank you for developing Clean Language for coaches and for your kindness and care in supporting me to discover who I really am and never judging even when I revealed an ugly side of my thoughts.

Caitlin Walker – author of *From Contempt to Curiosity – Creating the conditions for groups to collaborate* and the originator of Systemic Modelling – thank you for giving me the courage to show up in a group and be myself.

Mark Andrews – my beloved husband. Thank you for having the courage to join me on this journey. You inspire me to grow and love more deeply each and every day.

Paige and Liam – my children – you challenge me and you love me unconditionally all at the same time. I hope that one day I will master that very same skill that you so naturally have.

Linda, Carl and Dawn, my sister, brother and sister-in-law – thank you for showing up and taking the time to say you are proud of me and that you believe in me. I want you to know that actually hearing those words made all the difference.

My mum and dad – for your strength and tenacity to never give up in the face of adversity.

Karen Williams – Librotas book mentor, author and friend – for pushing me when I wanted to give up and for believing in me when I didn't. For constantly keeping me on track and ensuring that the book was aligned with my purpose and my message.

Louise Lubke Cuss my editor for gently sending each iteration back without judgement or contempt and slowly but surely helping me smooth off the rough edges to create a book that is consistent and readable.

Suzii Fido – thank you for translating my thoughts into the beautiful images throughout this book, for the cover and for all my social media promotions. Thank you for the times when I needed to download and you listened and encouraged.

Tom Hogben – thank you for consistently responding and engaging with my newsletters and reading the first draft. Your regular responses made me feel like I was not alone and that someone was listening.

Helen Holden – my bestie – thank you for keeping me grounded and making sure that I did not forget to stop and live life as well as plan for it.

Belinda Butler – my personal trainer, client and friend – thank you for teaching me to view my body without criticism and educating me that not all pain is an indicator that you should give up and that there is such a thing as a good stretch.

Sheryl Andrews – I want to thank myself. That might sound weird but I have needed and valued all this support and yet it is me that had to show up and do the work so for me it is important to acknowledge my part in this process.

Peer support – for everyone that has supported and encouraged me on line and off line. Thank you for your kindness. Every comment, every like and every share reminded me that my audience were waiting for me to speak.

Reviews

I was fortunate enough to be part of the team of proof readers that Sheryl asked to support her as she wrote this book. Having worked with Sheryl I can say she is one of the most giving people I have ever met and this book is a great example of her generosity. It provides straightforward, down to earth methods that make sense and are easy to implement. As a result of this book I have gained more confidence to stand up and say what I think and feel both at home and at work. It was great to be reminded that my opinion is just as important as anyone else's and to have practical ways to communicate it without the drama. I have been so inspired I am now looking to set up my own business.

Tom Hogben, Entrepreneur in the making

I love this book! When I trained as a coach I was amazed at how powerful the act of listening was and yet it was only available to those that decided to formally train as coaches and practitioners. Not any more thanks to Sheryl; you now have a valuable resource in your hands (and if you're a coach, you will still benefit from reading this book too).

I have gained great insights and questions to ask myself, my clients, and my family, from this book. Sheryl says when "you stop being curious, you stop listening". This is so true, and yet there are multiple reasons why we stop being curious. Sometimes, we are simply too tired. However, Sheryl recognises this, after having experienced it herself, and gives helpful tips and suggested actions to manage yourself during those times.

Sheryl suggests that listening to yourself without criticism allows you to listen to others without judgement or opinion. Imagine a world where you are no longer being held back by criticism, judgement or opinion. That is a world I want to live in.

Helen Monaghan, Finance coach and author of *Successful Business Minds* and *12 Steps to Improve your Cashflow.*

Introduction

Welcome to *Manage Your Critic – From Overwhelm to Clarity in 7 Steps. A practical guide for parents, managers and entrepreneurs.* Before we get started you might be thinking you don't fit into one of the titles – parent, manager or entrepreneur and maybe you don't. Maybe you call yourself a sole trader, self-employed, a founder or a business owner. Maybe you don't have children or lead a team. However, I do believe you will be someone that works hard to make a difference. That might be for your family, your team, your community and for those thinking a bit bigger you might be wanting to make a global difference. What I believe you and I may also have in common is that you are not driven by the money. Money however is one tool we can use to measure progress. Money is the currency that currently gives us more time to do the things we love and support the causes and people that matter to us most. Whatever title or role you give yourself I assume that you are here because you care and you want something to change.

After 25 plus years of motivating and inspiring others to create and manage change, I woke up realising that I was stuck going around in circles feeling like I wasn't getting anywhere. At my lowest point, I felt a complete failure and wondered why I was even bothering. I genuinely believed my mood swings and lack of consistency meant that my children would be better off without me and at the time it was my business that kept me focused and gave me hope. And when my business hit challenges it was my children that kept me focused. They are both so entwined and one supports the other. As I worked with my clients there was all the evidence I needed that it was possible to manage your critic. They were gaining clarity, confidence was growing and change definitely happened. I had to master taking my own advice, because whatever I was doing for them worked. In my frustration I often gave up hope and considered closing the business down, but something inside me said I wasn't to give up.

Over the years I have become aware that we all have a voice in our head and some have a critic that asks questions and challenges decisions. Then one day I noticed I had another voice. There was this little detective that loved to ask questions to understand how things worked. She had been paying attention to how I listened and what made me different. Every day investigating and collecting evidence of how I added value. When I started to give both the detective and the critic equal opportunity to be heard things changed.

At first I thought all I did was listen, then as the detective encouraged me to investigate and drilled down with more and more questions, I realised that not everyone listens like me, and not everyone pays attention to the same things that I do.

Once I understood how I do what I do, it made sense of so much and with this clarity my business partnerships and personal relationships started to flourish. When I was able to manage my critic all kinds of things happened – including writing this book. I had said all my life I wanted to write a book but something kept stopping me.

What I have come to realise is that as humans we are experiencing change all the time and we each have our own limit of how much change we can take. Ironically at the time I reached my limit, I had created three change programmes that helped my clients gain clarity and confidence. But because I had not taken the time to listen to my own advice I quickly moved from overwhelm to crisis.

Instead of managing my critic I was verbalising everything it had to say without really listening. Slowly but surely I shut down and eventually blocked out the voice of the detective and lost focus and purpose.

At home I was stuck, consistently complaining about what was not working and what I didn't want or didn't have or what wasn't fair. At work I thought I was wearing a good mask and that no one knew, but they could tell. I smiled, I was positive and I was still trying to help as many people as possible, often doing lots of work unpaid.

I had to change my focus to change the response. I had to change who and what I listened to. I had to become more strength and solution focused. I had to be willing to look in the mirror, manage my critic and then see and hear the good in myself. I had to give myself the same gift I gave my clients.

You might find yourself asking others for the answers, for advice, and searching for the clues outside of you and if that is working that is great. But if, like me, you get exhausted by helping everyone else and never seeming to find the answer for yourself maybe now is the time to stop searching outside and take a moment to really stop, reflect and really listen to what your critic is actually saying.

Listening isn't as easy as just being quiet. It is about the way you ask questions and what you ask questions of. It is about which words you reflect back and how you hear that information that will ultimately determine if you get to hear your own thoughts. Sometimes when others listen to us they interrupt us with their thoughts, ideas and suggestions. Instead of hearing yourself think you get the other person's opinion added to the pile of confusion you already had.

Many including me are guilty of expecting our family and friends to listen without any real consideration of how complex the skill of listening is. Many are unaware of how many hours of training professional listeners undergo and how often they practise to develop that skill.

It is my hope and aspiration that reading this book will give you more compassion and understanding when someone you love is not able to listen to you in the way you need and that you will finish this book with the skills to listen to yourself more effectively. I hope you will know that asking for help from those that are trained to listen and investing in developing your own listening skills is not a sign of weakness or a soft skill but more like a vital life-saving skill, that we all need to navigate change.

And I trust that you will listen to yourself better today than you did yesterday and then you will pay it forward: listening better each and every day to those that matter to your success and happiness.

Sheryl

The Strength and Solution Detective

Where to start

Part 1 – The Strength and Solution Detective

This section is about me, Sheryl Andrews, and how I became The Strength and Solution Detective. If you are the kind of person who wants to know who I am and what makes me the author tick, then you will start here.

Part 2 & 3 – Clarity and Confidence

These sections cover more of the practical processes and the theory behind why this listening is needed and what works.

Clarity – This section is about the 7 steps to C.L.A.R.I.T.Y. This is how I listen when I support my clients one to one to gain the clarity and confidence to create and manage change. It is a combination of the step by step process I went through as I trained to become a professional listener and some of my own lessons blended together. Each step will give you more self-awareness and practical tools to resource you to achieve success without stress. If you like to understand the process and the theory behind it, then you will start here.

Confidence – Once my business started to grow I started to run out of time and so I had to learn fast how to create a space where my clients could gain clarity in a group. Working with my clients we co-created the confidence model which forms the 10 step agenda I now follow when facilitating a group. So again if you want to know more about the theory and process behind confidence you will start here.

Part 4 – Workbooks

This is where I ask questions to encourage you to gain clarity and confidence of the change you want and practical ways to manage your critic. If you need to experience things in order to learn and you get bored or overwhelmed with too much detail, then this is where you will start.

Part 5 – Resources

This is where I have listed the resources and the books that I have referred to throughout the book.

Wherever you decide to start I hope you will come back and read the other sections, as each section gives you a new perspective.

Part I:
The Strength and Solution Detective

I just wanted everyone to be happy

For as long as I can remember I have always been someone that wanted people to get along and be happy. I only had to see someone roll their eyes, hear a huff, or gain a sense that something wasn't right, and my mind would start whirring with thoughts of how I could make things better.

I was happy to listen, to accommodate and to support. Then one day I realised I had become trapped behind the listening. It seemed safer to listen than to speak. I am a natural talker and trained listener but what many don't know is that even when I was talking, I was often only speaking about what I thought others wanted to hear. I wasn't necessarily expressing my own thoughts and feelings for fear of upsetting someone. I would backtrack, reframe and rephrase just because I had a 'sense' that someone disapproved.

Every now and then I would try to open up and actually say what I was thinking. But no one seemed to get me. They seemed more focused on criticising my grammar, my tone, my speed or my language. Few seemed able to actually hear what I was trying to say. Even fewer, if any, were able to acknowledge what I had said without giving me their suggestion. This left me feeling like everything I said was wrong and over time eroded my confidence in myself and my own opinion.

That is not to say that no one ever listened. Sometimes they would give me time to talk and they would nod politely and smile. In that moment it was lovely to offload. It felt good to share my thoughts without feeling judged. But when I had a real problem that I needed a solution to, I found that kind of listening didn't help. I would become exhausted by the sound of my own voice, saying the same thing over and over and nothing changing. Few people were skilled to listen long enough for me to gain clarity of my thinking.

I was perceived as sensitive and someone that took things too personally. I got that and I wanted to change. But I didn't know how to. I would ask people who seemed to have it mastered, and they would look at me as though I was mad and say something like "Stop overthinking it". Which really didn't help. I got it intellectually that I had to stop overthinking but emotionally I didn't know how to change and I didn't want to become insensitive and uncaring in the process.

Some were able to show empathy and would agree with me. They said they felt the same. There was a moment of relief to know it was not just me. That soon faded when I realised that just meant we were both stuck with the same problem and no solution.

I didn't understand why I couldn't express myself without getting emotional or why I was so sensitive to criticism.

Lots of things didn't make sense. I would hear one thing and see another. Take school for example. I had worked out how to pass exams and then became confused because some people considered me smart because I had these certificates. Yet I didn't feel smart because months, if not days, after passing them I could have sat the very same exams again and not remembered a thing.

How did that make me smart? What was that all about?

I often felt left out and misunderstood, and that pattern repeated itself time and time again.

That voice in my head, that I now lovingly refer to as my critic, thought there was something wrong with me and longed for me to be normal and to fit in. That was until I changed the way I listened. Then something quite magical happened.

The magic of listening

When I learned to listen to my critic with more compassion and without judgement I finally heard and understood my strengths and how to create solutions with those strengths in mind. I also understood why a skill or behaviour of mine could be a strength in one situation and potentially could really annoy somebody else in another. Finally understanding that everybody is somebody's difficult person at some point, took the pressure off me to please everyone all of the time and it encouraged me not to lose sight of when that same behaviour or attribute added value and was an asset.

If you are someone who is really sensitive and you care about helping others you might find yourself like me, trapped between doing what is right for you and what is right for them. Then your critic might come up with ideas of what you ought to do or what you should do or even what you could do. Until one day you find yourself stuck, unable to make a decision or take action for fear of upsetting someone. And you might, like me, find yourself resenting the fact that no one else seems to be bending over backwards to accommodate your needs and yet you are always making allowances for others.

When all this was happening in my head, I also became curious about how I could better motivate my clients who at the time were Slimming World members. I was fascinated by the fact that they would say one thing and do another. I noticed that many of those who referred to themselves as being slim in the past seemed more likely to maintain their target weight whereas those who had a critic that referred to them as having always been fat seemed more prone to lose the weight and then regain it.

I found myself having more and more conversations with my

clients about communication and relationships, discussing things such as: How do you manage meal times with a family when some refuse to buy into healthy eating? How do you reassure your partner that you are not going to leave just because you have lost weight and gained more confidence? I became interested in relationships and the relationship my clients had with food. I loved expressions like comfort food and comfort eating. It was my overthinking that would drive me to want to understand what this all meant.

So I signed up to find out more about coaching and attended my first coaching weekend in May 2006, which started a journey of learning how to ask more questions and change what I listened to and how I responded to what I heard.

My critic is now my trusted adviser who I seek counsel from and ask questions of. When I stopped trying to ignore or shut my critic down, I began to hear what it had been trying to say all along. In my experience my critic is either trying to protect me or someone else. And sometimes my critic is influenced by and operating on out-of-date data. Whenever I get curious I discover I have been saying or thinking things that are no longer true or based on an assumption so therefore were not a reality but simply a perception. All of which resulted in my critic perceiving danger when there really wasn't any.

Nowadays, listening gives me and my critic a chance to clarify and check out the evidence available to evaluate if the fear is valid. It is an opportunity to reboot and reset my internal systems with current information. This in turn improves my performance and my ability to communicate with those that matter to my success and happiness.

My critic

My critic used to show up in two forms. One that lived on my right shoulder, constantly twittering in my ear, telling me what I had done wrong and how I would fail. This was a small bug-like character that was quite shy. As I got to know him I discovered he is very risk averse and yet he thinks long and hard before speaking. He hates wasting time or money. So he is constantly scanning for potential problems. And there was this massive giant creature that stood just in front of me off to the right and when he spoke he was really loud and it made my whole body shake from head to toe, often resulting in me crying.

He didn't seem to think much before he spoke. He generally said things as they were from his map of the world without much concern for how that impacted me. When he criticised it was like I had been physically kicked in the stomach with a size 9 boot. As I listened to this critic I noticed a pattern. I was impacted more by criticism that came from people who I really cared about and whose opinion I truly valued. And unexpected criticism hit me the hardest. Then I noticed that when I criticised myself that reduced the risk of unexpected criticism. But it also made me sensitive to criticism, it eroded my self-confidence and it held me back from tuning into my strengths and my full potential and so that had to change.

Do I get upset by criticism now? Yes of course I do. I still get the odd wobble when I receive unexpected criticism but now I can evaluate it. I can ask questions to put the feedback into context and then I can make an informed decision. I can also park criticism that does not support my growth. I no longer spend hours or days mulling over a comment. Instead I process it, accept the learning and then let it go.

I was able to make these changes because of the training

that I did to become a coach. By changing the way I listened, I changed my focus and that changed the response. By learning to ask more questions and noticing patterns I started to understand what triggered my critic to have a concern. This gave me the insight I needed to hear, understand and eventually manage my critic.

Ironically I had been doing this for my clients for years and it took a family crisis for me to really stop and take my own advice.

My daughter was just 16 when in a moment of despair and exhaustion I gave her an ultimatum and she decided that she would rather be homeless than live with me. Her version of the event is that I kicked her out. And I do understand that for her I didn't give her any choices she could live with, so from her map of the world she was made homeless. We had been rowing nearly every night for what had seemed like forever. I tried to listen. I tried to give advice and no matter what I did she was still angry with me. I felt like I could never get anything right. I spent all of my time trying to make her happy without truly understanding what was making her unhappy. I assumed it was me. And I had reached the point where I truly believed she would be better off without me. At the time I was marketing myself as a "mums and daughters" relationship coach. I felt such a fraud because I could not achieve the same results for myself as I did my clients. I knew talking it through with someone who was outside of the system would help me make sense of it, but I was too scared to open up and admit I was failing; besides, I thought I should know better.

I had broken down in tears and cried so hard one night that I could not breathe. Then I looked up and saw the concern in my young son's face and knew I had to get help. Trying to do this on my own was not working. In a desperate attempt I found myself calling Parent Line, a free helpline that was available then. I finally gave myself the gift of being heard without judgement. I allowed myself the freedom to cry and share the pain of my failure without fear of being misunderstood. But it had taken a crisis before I did.

The young man on Parent Line, who could not have been much more than 20, listened as I sobbed about what a failure I was. I asked questions like how come I have helped my clients grow their business, buy new cars, move house, go on holiday and have better relationships at home and I can't do it for myself.

That evening the young man listened with compassion and without judgement. He knew he was not responsible for solving my problems; he was trained to listen and he knew he just had to listen long enough for me to gain a new perspective. He spoke with a kind and gentle tone that pulled me in and settled me down. Slowly but surely my breathing became more settled and the crying eased, and he asked me a question that changed my focus.

He asked, "What would you tell your clients to do?"

In that moment I realised that I had been so focused on my daughter and what she needed that I had not listened to what I wanted or what support I needed.

I would ask my clients:

- What would you like to have happen?
- How do you need to be for that to happen?
- And what kind of support would you need?

By asking these questions I changed their focus, from the other person to themselves and their own needs. By setting them up for success they could manage their critic and that resourced them to change their focus when listening to their daughter. Sometimes the daughter would respond differently or the mother would notice that even though the daughter stayed the same her own response was different. She was now calmer or less stressed and less worried.

With each iteration the mother became more able to listen

without fear of failure or feelings of guilt and together they were able to co-create a solution that worked for them.

That day I started to attend my own programmes with the love and support of my team and my husband. Ironically, I had always had people around me willing to support me, but my critic said I would lose face if I asked for help. I was the business owner and the leader – I had to stay strong and I believed I had to have it all together to keep others motivated and inspired. I had by now trained four facilitators to run Step by Step Listening group clarity sessions and my husband who is also a certified facilitator. Not to mention all the friends and family members who would have done anything to help if only I'd asked. You see, on the outside everyone saw a happy successful businesswoman, and few knew how I really felt inside.

I knew I had to give myself time to really slow my thinking down and actually listen to understand what I wanted. I had to listen to my critic and give him time to express his concerns. All the time remembering to challenge the information in a loving and compassionate way. With each iteration I was checking if the thought was reasonable or realistic. What I noticed is that I rarely noticed what was working or what had worked and so I had to develop my 'What's working muscle' and start noticing my own strengths. The more I did this, the easier it became to manage my critic.

I also noticed that I had to specifically take time to pay attention to the changes no matter how small and to fully celebrate and truly acknowledge it. I remember being really proud of the fact that I had managed to listen to my daughter for two minutes longer today than yesterday before she became frustrated and defensive. I would notice which questions worked for her and which didn't and gradually step by step we worked our way back to a loving bond.

I wanted to be able to listen to her all the time without judgement, just like I did my clients, but it was not instant. Noticing the small gradual increments of change kept me motivated to keep going because it updated my internal system and reassured my critic we were making progress and that this was not a waste of time. When I had clarity about the solution I wanted, I was able to stay focused on that outcome and I was more resourceful.

And with each step in the right direction and with greater clarity, my confidence grew. I should point out that I did need to recruit the help of some really good friends and family members. I asked them to ask me: "What is working?" or "What would I like to have happen?" if they heard me complaining about what was not working or what I didn't want. The more I noticed the small changes the more changes seemed to happen and my critic became quieter and less insistent.

Then I noticed that I had another character who lived in my head: it was a little detective – this detective was obsessed with evidence to support beliefs and rules.

Whether I was being criticised internally or externally, the detective was naturally drawn to ask more questions to clarify and understand: What specifically had been seen and heard to support that thought or feeling? This character was created as a direct result of training to become a coach and learning how to ask good questions and improving my listening skills.

As I listened some more I recognised that I also had a gold cheerleader who looks a bit like one of those Oscar awards, only she is shaking two gold pompoms. She lives in my heart and jumps into action when clients lose sight of their success. The cheerleader notices if things change for the better or worse but then sends the detective off to collect more clues of how this situation can be used as a strength. She is proactive to prove you matter and she hates it if you lose sight of how you add value.

When I was at my lowest point and asking questions like "How come I can motivate and inspire others but I can't seem to do that for myself?" my detective noticed that the cheerleader rarely stood up for me. She never noticed what I did well; she was always focused on what was happening externally and how well everyone else was doing but rarely transferred that same skill internally.

When my detective asked me, what would I like to have happen? I realised that I wanted to be more strength and solution focused. I wanted to notice my own strengths more and to pay attention to what was happening when I was working at my best.

That is when the detective and cheerleader started to work in harmony and 'The Strength and Solution Detective' was born. The Strength and Solution Detective collects evidence with a particular curiosity to understand and collect the clues that prove how someone adds value and makes a difference. Because of the unique way I hear and process information my strengths will always be up for criticism by someone at some point. With the right support I have overcome my sensitivity to criticism and I am learning how to be more sensitive when giving feedback to others when something is not working for me. You see, whilst I am sensitive, I could be equally insensitive when my thoughts and feelings finally exploded out of me.

With this understanding of myself, my mind became calmer and I gained clarity. With clarity there was now space for confidence to grow, and change happened. I was by now more resourced to manage the unexpected criticism and change that life so often throws our way.

All of this was achieved because of a beautiful and magical listening skill called Clean Language that has transformed the way I listen to myself and others. I could not have discovered these internal resources, if it were not for this listening skill, and this in turn has given me courage to stand up and ask for my needs to be met.

By learning to be more curious and listen without judgement, I have learned to make sense of why I do what I do. I now understand how my memory works, and why I could not retain the information from those exams – and why I remembered in technicolour every time someone criticised me but I rarely remembered when someone said something nice about me.

I also know now why I was not being heard and understood. With this new information I can and do have the resources to achieve success without stress. I now know how to change my focus to change the response.

I no longer feel the need to be happy and positive all of the time to please everyone else. I too can give my face a rest and have a sad face if I so desire.

I accept that sometimes life is pants. People die and beautiful things come to an end. I now listen to and give every emotion the space to be heard and if my peer support is busy I do pay for listening.

I know now that I am more likely to be sensitive if I am overtired and exhausted so I focus on what I need to work, learn and live at my best. I have created a business that allows me time to have fun and rest. I also know that when I lack clarity or have any self-doubt then any criticism from others has a greater impact, so I make it a habit to check in with myself regularly to ensure I always know what I want and what works for me.

The more I do this work, the more often I can show up as the best version of myself.

I am perfectly imperfect which makes me just perfect, as are you.

I regularly sit with my 'Strength and Solution Detective' and chat about the evidence he has collected and we celebrate all kinds of change.

I am still a sensitive person and I still get upset when I am criticised, only now it's not an emotional meltdown that makes others fearful of giving me feedback. Now it is more like a little tremor inside and I can take a deep breath, ask questions and listen to the criticism. Then I can make an informed decision based on fact not assumption.

Over the years I discovered I had built metaphorical and physical protection systems around me in an attempt to protect myself from being criticised. It turned out that I had built a fortress to keep me safe, which became a prison and limited my ability to truly live and love. Every day that I spend listening to my critic, I am able to break down yet another barrier and give myself more and more freedom to live my life to the full.

My large critic is now out front with a massive smile just warning me of danger and giving me choice. My little critic spends much of his time travelling in a metaphorical backpack on my back and occasionally will pop up and sit on my shoulder for a chat.

My cheerleader is now virtually full size inside me and her gold heart shines out in all that I do. The Strength and Solution Detective is inside and out, proactively spreading the word and encouraging others to collect evidence and notice patterns with the purpose and intention of reminding us all that we matter and we each have our own unique story to share. Within every story are the clues of our strengths and how we add value and make a difference.

Managing change

Change is something that is constant and yet few take the time to listen to their thoughts or give themselves time to express their feelings. Life is so fast paced it is like there is no time allowed to be sad or even over joyous. Each emotion, feeling or belief is only given a fleeting moment to be heard and can so often be misunderstood in the process. This is when your critic can become unsettled and starts questioning whether you are safe, and I believe that is when the critic associates change as something to be fearful of.

To break this pattern of behaviour you may need to ask for help and some don't feel okay about doing that, be it physical help or emotional help. It's as though our generation have worked so hard for independence we have lost sight of the beauty of partnership and collaboration. Personally, I was okay paying for help but not so good at being offered help. When I was paying for help I was able to justify it to myself as helping them out which conveniently short circuited the need to admit I needed help. When someone offered to help me, I felt vulnerable and questioned what they had heard and seen and worried I had come across as needy. I was afraid I looked weak and like I couldn't cope on my own. It never occurred to me that someone had simply seen an opportunity to do more of what they loved or that they wanted to be of value and contribute.

As humans, I believe, we underestimate how much change impacts us, and with support it can be so much easier. That support might be the help of someone who is trained to listen and gives you the chance to share the load emotionally or it could be physically.

Prior to the breakdown in my relationship with my teenage

daughter, I had not fully appreciated how much change I had personally experienced and how not asking for help had hindered me when it came to supporting her through her teens.

I was so busy supporting my clients and my family I neglected to stop and consider what help I needed and who could I collaborate with to gain that help. Instead I would insist on paying for every bit of help I did have and seemed unaware of the debt accruing. Insisting on paying full price for everything in an attempt to show them how much I valued them. I was however more than happy to work for free to help others.

As a result, I was not making good business decisions; they were very much emotionally driven. I thought it was normal for a new business to be in debt and so didn't really question it.

When I reflect now I can see over 6–7 years just how much change I had experienced and I genuinely believe I could have avoided the crisis with my daughter had I asked for help sooner.

We all go through change but I wonder if you really have noticed how much these events impact your clarity, your confidence and therefore your critic. When I hit crisis point, I took my own advice and I gave myself the gift of professionally trained listeners who gave me space and time to focus on understanding what I wanted and needed. This was not about what my business needed or what my family needed but what I needed. Although what I needed did include a successful business and happy confident family, it was about me. I actually found it quite hard at first to think about what I wanted for me personally. I explored what kind of business, what kind of clients and even what kind of marriage I needed for me to be at my best.

To put things into context, below are a list of the key changes that I experienced that I am aware impacted me. Some of the changes ate away at my self-worth and my self-confidence and yet there were some really positive changes that seemed to go unnoticed and uncelebrated as well.

July 2003

My first marriage came to an end and I felt a complete failure. I can now look back and see that having children and then the death of my father-in-law did have a massive impact on us both. Neither of us was equipped to communicate what we wanted so we just complained about each other instead. I had a belief that marriage was for life and I was the one who said enough is enough and so I was doing one thing but believing another.

May 2005

Aged 37 and with two young children I found myself back on the dating scene. After two years of dating experiences from hell, I gave up and decided to accept I was happier when I was not dating. Then just as I said that I met Mark, my now husband, soulmate and best friend. We had lots of fun and we had some challenges. Neither of us had any experience of divorced families with both our parents staying married. So we were learning by trial and error what worked and what didn't to manage our new relationship, five children and two Jack Russells, whilst running two homes and both working full time. Although I was self-employed and therefore I could be more flexible with 'when' I worked I still had to do the work consistently to generate income.

July 2005

I lost contact with my one and only best friend at the time. I called her, I texted her, I emailed and put notes through the door but nothing – she just ignored me. We had known each other for 10 years and then nothing. I didn't know why she had stopped communicating so it didn't make sense and the children would ask constantly after her. I had never had a best friend and it was a massive loss. I am glad to say three years later we were reunited and we are the best of friends still.

May 2006

I became curious about how I could support my clients better and attended my first coaching weekend which opened my mind to a new way of thinking and a new way of listening. I realised what I wanted more than anything was to be a good mum and that getting divorced and buying my ex-husband out was the most important thing for me to do. That weekend I signed up and invested £3000 in a personal performance coaching diploma which would be the first of a series of investments to improve my ability to listen without judgement or assumption.

September 2006

I changed from self-employed franchisee to full time employed as Area Manager with Slimming World and now I was supporting 25 franchisees to grow their businesses. My ex-husband had started to come into the house at unexpected times like 6am or 9pm, creeping in and whispering in my ear: "Just so you don't forget I still own half the house." This intimidation motivated me to take an employed role with guaranteed money so that I could buy him out.

Two weeks after I started my new role, my mum was diagnosed with terminal cancer. We had never really been able to communicate and we often finished conversations feeling frustrated. Mark at the time was working away Monday to Friday and whilst he was brilliant at keeping in touch and listening over the phone I was pretty much a single parent and on my own. During this time, I was probably my most efficient. I had to keep the income coming in, I had to be there for my children, but nothing was going to stop me spending 4 hours a day at the hospital with my mum. I learned a lot about time management and focus during this period of my life.

November 2006

Mum died 30th November 2006, which hit me really hard. We had sat to the early hours of the morning talking and we had finally learned to listen without judgement or criticism. She had shared her thoughts and we had for the first time had honest heart centred conversations with only one purpose. We wanted the other person to know how much they were loved and valued. We wanted to apologise for the times we had not said what we were thinking and we had not expressed our love effectively. Just as she died I felt loved. I had always known I was loved but never quite felt it. The following year I buried my head in work.

July 2007

Mark moved in and sadly for us the two older children, that had lived with him, decided not to live with us. I felt like it was all my fault and that had an impact on our relationship. It wasn't the happy family scenario we had dreamed of.

May 2008

I coped as many do and used work as a distraction, thinking if I could earn more money I could make things better. Instead I burnt myself out and hit crisis point. I was by now working 70 hours a week and had lost the art of saying no or delegation that had served me so well when Mum was in hospital. Eventually as I lay in Mark's arms in floods of tears, he asked me what I wanted and my reply was, "I want to be a stay at home mum." That day I quit my full time job.

August 2008

Mark and I were married which was magical and with it brought more changes, the change of name being just one. And now for the first time since I was 14 years old I was financially dependent on someone else. The wedding plans had kept me busy at first but I soon found myself being bored and frustrated once Mark and the children went back to school and work. I really struggled to know my value without a salary. Cleaning windows and cooking meals didn't fulfil me and I felt like something was missing.

December 2008

When I had signed up for the diploma in May 2006, I had two years to complete it. Because of everything that was happening I had procrastinated and kept putting it on the back burner. Thankfully the training company was really good when I explained my circumstances and they gave me an extension. In December I achieved a distinction in personal performance coaching. The last module was all about how to launch a coaching business and almost by accident Step by Step Listening was born. By now I had adjusted my goal to being a really good working mum. For the first two years I networked and the business grew steadily. I love networking and connecting people. I even won Networking Champion of the Year in 2009. In winning this award it did highlight how much money I had made for others and my critic was not happy with how much I had made in comparison.

March 2010

During my training months, I had been coaching Mark and it turned out he was fed up with travelling and being away Monday to Friday. That resulted in him applying for a job locally that would mean he would be home every night. Like many new roles there was a probation period and when it came to the end of that period Mark wasn't happy and they parted company. They were not a company that knew how to maximise his strengths and he really wasn't reaching his full potential. I had it as part of my vision that we would work together so we took advantage of this opportunity and Mark joined me in the business. The learning we got from that is a book in itself.

The same month my youngest started to have difficulties with school and the net result was I agreed to home school him from age 12. The house now felt full with both my husband and my son at home all day. I had no space to breathe or collect my thoughts. And my daughter who was by now at college often felt excluded as she was the only one leaving the house each day. We had to make changes financially as we adjusted to the new situation, which really did impact everyone.

I was now effectively my husband's boss as he sat waiting for me to lead and delegate tasks. I was my son's teacher and he needed work each day and I had no idea what I was doing. I started to feel the pressure not only financially but emotionally to provide for everyone. It was a lot to handle.

I had been the main wage earner before in my first marriage, so that in itself was not a problem, but I was employed then so the marketing and the accounts were taken care of and all I had to do was show up and do my thing which I did really well. I earned bonuses that told me that my employer was happy with my work. I had always been a mum that was proactive to support my children at school and I loved sitting down with homework etc but home schooling to GCSE level with a memory like mine was a whole new ball game. I should point out that I didn't manage this. My son virtually taught himself and he took himself to night school aged 16–17 to do his exams.

It is not surprising when I look back that I wasn't coping well with my daughter as she returned home each night with her fears and frustrations, that I interpreted as attitude. I had been listening to and managing the needs and expectations of my clients all day and I was trying to ensure that my husband and son were both motivated and had enough to do. I would then go out networking keeping that positive smile on for everyone else, but inside I was feeling so overwhelmed and such a failure. There never seemed to be any respite for me. No time to process my own thoughts and feelings.

February 2011

In a moment of despair, I kicked my daughter out aged 16 or, as I prefer to say, I gave her an ultimatum and she chose to leave. I thought she would miss home and come running back but she never did and that feedback was tough to take. To know that your own child would rather be with strangers and be in danger than be with you. My trainer once said that if 10 of your team say you are rude, no matter what your own perception of yourself is, then you are rude. No matter how much I thought I was doing the best I could, this feedback meant that my best was not good enough.

Don't wait for crisis

I now recognise that I didn't take time to process and understand how I felt about the changes as they happened. My head was constantly full and I was trying to manage the needs of everyone else but rarely taking care of myself.

My critic said, "If you speak up and show yourself to be vulnerable then people won't respect you and then not only will you fail at home, you will also fail in business too."

I was devastated that my first marriage failed and I know that made me doubt my worth. I was heartbroken to lose my mum just as I had learned how to listen to her without judgement. Work and my salary became a way of feeling of value and a place where I seemed to get the rules and I had felt safe. Becoming an entrepreneur with no guaranteed income and many changes, I lost a major stabiliser in my life. Income, routine, structure and support were things I had taken for granted at work and I needed to recreate for myself.

My relationship with Mark has always been easy but it was challenging at times to balance the needs of our children and we didn't always get it right. Home schooling was the right decision but it was petrifying to break the rules and do things differently.

And despite all that I knew that setting up my own business was the right thing to do. It gave me flexibility to be a good working mum and an opportunity to experience a life without limits. I could choose my clients, my time and my salary. And I had no idea just how much that would challenge me. I had not realised how little I knew about how to run a business. I had been in a business but never really had to know how it was all working. I just turned up and did my part and got paid.

At first I did really well. They say ignorance is bliss and it seemed the more I learned the more I doubted myself. My critic would be hearing all the different ways to grow a business and would challenge me, questioning whether what I was doing was right. Then I became torn between my role as entrepreneur and mother never really sure if I was focusing on the right thing.

I had worked for people and with people and I had even been self-employed before, but that was with a franchise which meant they had already created the systems and processes and I had been employed for my specific skill set. I had not fully appreciated the systems and processes needed to make a business run smoothly. And I had no idea of my own internal systems and processes that could be used to create systems for my own business with my strengths in mind. I had always loved selling but I was selling something or someone else. When you own your own company you have to sell yourself, and how can you do that if your critic keeps telling you that you're getting it wrong? If you don't believe in you how is anyone else going to? At first I sold coaching; I now know that was a distraction. Then I sold Clean Language. But I soon found that people either didn't know what it was or were simply averse to talking or anything that might be in any way therapy-like or navel gazing. Then I paid attention to my own unique process and how I worked, and writing this book was my vehicle to gain clarity and confidence in myself. It's a tool and resource to build my business, and now I am confident to sell and serve because I know what I do, why I do, and how it works.

The signs were there so much earlier, if only I had taken the time to listen and manage my critic then maybe, just maybe, my daughter and I would not have hit crisis before I stopped and really listened. Maybe just maybe my own mum and I could have had those perfect mum and daughter days I had always dreamed of.

Maybe, just maybe, I would have learned how to collaborate and ask for help and my business would have been financially successful sooner. But though I can't go backwards, I can continue to learn and grow and share with others.

The one thing that I did learn is that entrepreneurs were more likely to invest in themselves before they hit crisis. They could see how clarity and confidence could help them increase profits and efficiency.

Families, it seemed on the other hand (including me), would struggle for far longer on their own in private and would often only reach out when their teens had attempted to commit suicide or were self-harming. Or their marriage had come to an end.

Once I was clear who I wanted to help it became clear that working with more businesses meant I could prevent crisis both at work and home for more people.

Over the years one common pattern showed up. Mums and dads who came to me for family relationship stuff were far more likely to resolve things if they did not have any other additional stress from work. That's when I changed my focus and started to work with entrepreneurs. My definition of an entrepreneur is someone that owns their business but has a bigger purpose than just making a profit; they want to make a difference. For some that difference is with their own family and children and for others it is a global difference. And it is knowing that I have given someone that space to grow and do more of what they love that really makes my heart expand.

I truly believe entrepreneurs with passion and purpose can redistribute the world's wealth by creating work environments that work with us and nature, not against us.

From sole trader to supported trader

I have been self-employed in some capacity or other since 1999 except for the short break when I took the employed role from September 2006 to May 2008. What I recognise now is that when things were going well at work I was more resourced to be present and patient at home.

Once I was out of crisis I had to really look at my business and understand where it was haemorrhaging money. I had to understand who I was going to partner with and create collaborations. And like dating, I had heard many horror stories about partnerships that went wrong, and so again I had to gain clarity about what I wanted and manage my critic. I had to be able to motivate and inspire but also have the courage to speak up when it was not working.

Being a sole trader was absolutely the best decision I have ever made and when I became a supported trader it transformed the way I felt about myself, my strengths and my contribution to the world. I no longer felt alone. It stopped being hard work, things started to make sense, and I was able to show up and do my best work. By finding the right people to collaborate with and talk to in confidence about the things that were not working as well as the things that were, I was able to grow. Today I recognise that I am an entrepreneur with a global mission to change the way the world listens – breaking down barriers that prevent connection and collaboration.

I hope this guide and the stories inspire you to change the way you listen to your critic and that you finish the book with clarity about what you want and the confidence to make it happen. I hope you will join us on line and share your success and how you celebrated them.

Part 2: Clarity

Introduction

When you are in overwhelm you may have lots of thoughts and possibilities. Sometimes those thoughts are fear driven and sometimes dream and vision driven. But without clarity you will find yourself stuck. Slowing life down for just a moment and learning to listen can and will create change.

In this section I will be sharing with you 7 steps I use to gain clarity and some of the things I am considering when I am listening to myself and my clients.

7 steps to Clarity

Step 1 **C** = Curiosity
Step 2 **L** = Language
Step 3 **A** = Attention
Step 4 **R** = Reflection
Step 5 **I** = Intention
Step 6 **T** = Trust
Step 7 **Y** = You

Curiosity – *"A willingness to see the same thing from a different perspective"*

Your ability to ask questions and then listen without judgement will determine your level of curiosity and therefore your ability to manage your critic and gain clarity. This first step therefore focuses on questioning and listening skills whilst sharing some simple models that make sense of why sometimes you may struggle to stay curious even when you want to.

Language – *"Your words and language matter – pay attention and notice patterns"*

Once you know how to listen better you can start to refine what you ask questions of and you can also be curious about words and language that impact your clarity and confidence and therefore hinder your ability to listen and remain curious.

Attention – *"The quality of your attention determines the quality of your thinking"*

Everyone has a certain perspective and perception that they are more drawn to. Your natural way of working and thinking will often represent your strengths and those same strengths can show up as a challenge. Learning to notice where your attention is and then developing your skill to give all information equal opportunity can bring balance to your system. This is not about changing who you are – it is about changing your focus to change the response.

Reflection – *"Sometimes the answers are in your past and sometimes they are right in front of you"*

Sometimes no matter how hard you listen clarity doesn't emerge. As the saying goes "You don't know what you don't know." This is when you might have to look outside of you for the answers. Maybe the evidence is in the way others respond or the way others behave and it might be in your past. And you might need to ask for evidence based feedback to explore how your behaviour is being interpreted and the impact it is having on others.

Intention – *"Communicate from a place of good intent and love"*

Even with great evidence based feedback and great listening skills, if you are communicating from a place of contempt or judgement of yourself or others it is unlikely that your communication will land or get the response you want. In this section we explore ways to identify when you are in drama and how to get out of it.

Trust – *"The firm belief in the reliability, truth or ability of someone or something"*

Really understanding your own step by step process for doing things like how you make decisions, how you plan and how you manage time can all contribute to a better understanding of yourself and therefore increased trust in the way you work and your knowledge and experience. This section explores different ways to develop awareness of your own processes.

You – *"You matter and you are on purpose – your why is your lighthouse guiding you in every decision and every thought"*

And after all that, perhaps your critic still thinks why are you bothering and still questioning what is your life all about and what is your purpose. This section is about exploring your why, and ensuring the whole of you and your story are heard by sharing resources that help you be you without apology, and how to tell your story without the drama or blame.

Before we get started I want to invite you to take a minute now to work through a few questions to settle your critic so that we can work at our best together. To do that I want to share with you two short processes called 'Setting you up for success' and 'Space matters'.

Setting you up for success

- What would you like to have happen when you finish reading this book?
- What is happening when you are reading and learning at your best?
- How do you need to be for reading and learning to be like that?
- Is there any kind of resource or support you need right now to be curious and open to learning something new?

Take a moment and write your answers down, then pick one or two words out of your own response and be curious:

What would you hear and see that would tell you that is happening?

For example:

What I would like to have happen is to change the way the world listens one person at a time.

I could then pick two words which I am drawn to. In this instance I am drawn to 'listen' and 'person'.

I would then ask:

What kind of listen is that listen?

And what kind of person is that person?

I might also get curious and ask questions about the word 'change'.

What kind of change is that change?

Once you have your statement and you have chosen your words, then write down your response to those extra questions. Be interested in any new insights you gain, if any.

Space matters

Take a moment now to be curious about where you have decided to place yourself to read this book.

Notice if this is where you always read this kind of book. Do you have different spaces for different kinds of books? By paying attention to patterns of which spaces work best for which task, you increase your awareness of what you need to set yourself up for success.

I recently worked with a client who said "As I drove over here it became clearer what I had to do." Then later on she mentioned that "When I walked the other day the problem seemed to sort itself out." By asking questions and putting her attention on the fact that she was moving when clarity came, means now if she is stuck with a problem she knows to get up and go for a walk or a drive and invariably the answer comes.

Have you ever experienced leaving a room to get something, then when you get there you can't remember why? Yet when you walk back to where you started you suddenly remember. That is because your brain stores information inside you and outside of you and your environment is stimulating your thinking all of the time.

Another client had noticed she suddenly felt restless and less productive. She thought it was the drain of training a new member of the team. And whilst this was taking lots of energy, the thing that was making a massive difference was that she had moved her desk to fit this team member in and now her desk did not face the window. The view of outside was what motivated her and empowered her to work at her best, and losing that view was impacting her ability to think.

You are processing information around you all of the time, even if you don't think you are. When you become curious about what is happening when it works for you and what is happening when it doesn't, you can start to create your own blueprint of which spaces work best for which kind of thinking or work. For now, I want you to be curious about what kind of space works best for you to read and learn.

Notice if you put up with the wrong space or make do even though your critic has tried to point out you are in the wrong space. Maybe your critic worries about how changing space might impact others? Perhaps your critic doesn't want you to be a nuisance or make a fuss? Pay attention: there are often two critics. One that is worried about what you need and one that worries about how your behaviour or actions impact others.

- Are you in the right space now?
- Are you facing in the right direction?

Actually stop and notice what is happening to you physically. Notice how you feel. Do you feel silly or impatient? Do you feel this is a waste of time? Be willing to stop and just notice what is happening for you right now.

Did you change space or adjust yourself? Even if only ever so slightly?

Notice that little change and acknowledge what works for you right now.

- Are you at the right angle?
- Are you at the right height?

These are the kind of questions I am going to ask. It is always my intention to take you to the edge of your current thinking and to give you new insights and a new perspective. I do understand that it takes courage to look at things differently. This is an invitation to be courageous. Pick up your strength and solution detective hat, your magnifying glass, and proactively notice and collect the clues and evidence of your strengths and what makes you amazing. (And notice if your critic just said "Yeah right" or any other snide remark doubting your value. You do matter and you make a difference. Be willing to notice how and why.)

Whilst this book is very much focused on managing your inner critic, the process is virtually identical when it comes to managing those that criticise you. You have to be able to listen to them without judgement or assumption, and the best way I know how to achieve that is to learn to listen and manage your own inner critic first.

You will be training yourself to collect the clues and evidence of your strengths and how to be more solution focused. You will begin to pay exquisite attention to patterns and step by step you will unravel what has been holding you back. You will start to notice how you work and think. This information will help you understand your very own unique blueprint of how you do you.

Your purpose for listening is not to make change happen but to be curious about the change you want and to observe change as it happens. How you ask questions, and what you ask questions of, can and will change your focus. By noticing what you say and think you give yourself the opportunity to truly listen to yourself. Please celebrate any change that moves you closer to managing your critic. Notice when you have more clarity and when confidence is growing. The celebration can be as simple as a thumbs-up or a cheeky smile in the mirror. It might be a journal or sharing the change with a friend. It doesn't matter how you celebrate, but it does matter that you do take time to celebrate. By physically acknowledging when you are making progress you give your critic new information.

Whilst the process of CLARITY is a step by step process I also see it more like the diagram opposite, where curiosity is at the heart of it. Be playful and feel free to hop from one step to another in any particular order always being mindful of the whole process.

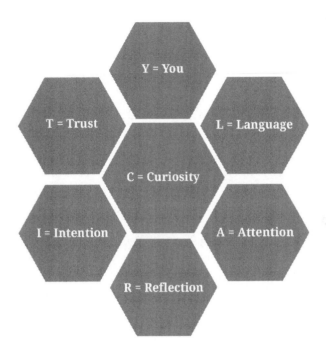

Step 1: Curiosity

"A willingness to see the same thing from a different perspective"

You will need to be willing to develop your detective skills and pay attention to patterns and clues. Gaining clarity and learning to manage your critic can be a bit like untangling a ball of wool. Sometimes you are able to pull one strand and the whole ball instantly unravels. So sometimes you can ask one question and the answer instantly appears and everything makes sense and you are left with clarity.

Other times asking questions can cause more confusion for a moment and it's like the ball of wool becomes more tangled and the knot becomes tighter. You have to be patient and persistent and willing to fiddle around a bit to find another way in. Your ability to stay curious and ask more questions will allow you, piece by piece, to unravel the ball of wool and gain the clarity you are looking for to manage your critic. In this chapter we will be exploring what might prevent you from being curious, questioning skills and listening skills.

What rules might prevent curiosity?

Many of my clients really believed they couldn't read because they were slower than other children at school and others believed they couldn't write because a grandparent sent back letters with red pen and corrections.

You need to be open to asking and to being asked questions. Your critic might truly believe you are not intelligent enough to ask good questions. Your critic might have a rule that only smart people can be curious. I want you to know that you are enough and you can do this. We are all geniuses in our own unique way and you are very capable of learning to listen with the purpose of understanding your own mind.

Be curious: What rules do you have around your ability to learn or to remember that might prevent you from staying engaged with the process?

What rules do you have about emotions and feelings that might prevent you from exploring how you feel about something?

Be open minded and willing to explore.

Throughout this section I will be asking you questions and sometimes you might not know the answers immediately. I invite you to make a note and over the next few days pay attention and notice if the answer emerges, and if it doesn't then that is information in itself. You will now know that you don't know and you can choose to find out or not. The choice is yours.

Notice where you are when you discover the answer. Who are you with? And what happens just before the answer emerges?

Your brain and curiosity

The brain has a brilliant mechanism to keep you safe and that in turn can prevent you from sustaining curiosity. The Triune Brain model developed by Paul Maclean was a model that I came across when working with Caitlin Walker, author of *From Contempt to Curiosity – Creating conditions for groups to collaborate* and it quickly transformed how I managed my critic. It makes sense of why you might get distracted or feel unsettled and stop listening and therefore stop being curious. At a very basic level, we are animals. We need to know we are safe. Do we fit in? And what are the rules? We also need to be fed and well rested to be able to think clearly and to learn.

The Triune Brain

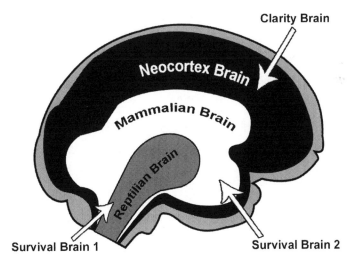

In this model there are 3 parts of the brain referred to as:

1. Reptilian
2. Mammalian
3. Neocortex

I tend to refer to the reptilian and mammalian brain as survival brains and the neocortex as the clarity brain.

Reptilian brain – survival brain I

The reptilian brain is located at the back of your head. It's attached to the spinal cord and is about the size of your fist. This was the first brain to be developed and it is about our basic animal instincts to survive and keep us safe. It will respond automatically and you might see and hear behaviour of fight, flight or freeze when you feel threatened or unsafe.

When this brain first evolved we had to run from or fight predators, and whilst that can happen in our everyday life now the reality is that for the vast majority of us it is rarely life threatening; it just feels like it might be. That is when this part of the brain can kick in, driven by old and out-of-date data. The response can be quick and automatic, pumping adrenaline from our clarity brain to our extremities such as hands and feet. Giving us the power to run or fight.

It could be as simple as not knowing when you are going to be able to eat or drink next, meaning your reptilian brain might start to become agitated.

It could be fear of where your next client is coming from or how you will pay your mortgage.

Can you think of a time when your reptilian brain kicks in?

Have you noticed when you are in flight, fight or freeze?

My clients have said things like:

"The other day I couldn't find the words. My client questioned why I did something and I didn't know. I felt stupid for not knowing what or why I had just said or did what I did. It was autopilot and I didn't really think about it, it just felt right and when questioned I can't really articulate what I did or why. I remember feeling like I did at school as though I had been caught out or failed a test. I just froze and said nothing for what felt like ages."

"I found myself snapping at my partner and even I know that I am being unreasonable."

"When I am at networking events – I just want to get out and for the whole experience to be over."

Have a think now about a time when you are in flight, flight or freeze.

What happens just before fight, flight or freeze?

What does your reptilian brain need to hear and see to be settled and to know you are safe?

Mammalian brain – survival brain 2

The mammalian part of the brain covers the reptilian brain and this is where the rules are stored and where we create an understanding of social norms and how we do things around here. In my lifetime so many rules have been challenged and changed and I am sure you are no different.

This part of the brain, although focused on understanding the rules, is again very much based on protection and survival. What are the rules? How do I need to behave to fit in and survive?

You might have experienced this when in a training session. Perhaps you have a question and you start to wonder when is the right time to ask your questions. Do you worry about interrupting or talking too much or not enough? Your mammalian brain will be counteracting preventing you from really listening because it wants to know the rules so that it knows you are safe.

When I recently attended Systemic Modelling training with Clean Learning, Caitlin Walker talked about 3 kinds of rules. These really made sense of so much for me and have really helped me to have more fun exploring why my critic has kicked off.

1. **Shared rules** – these are the rules you share openly. Maybe you express them verbally or perhaps in a written contract. You might set out what you want and what you expect from others and you share your expectations.

2. **Unspoken or internal rules** – these are the rules you say in your head and you don't say out loud. You might find your

critic saying things like "That's not fair" or "That's not right" but you don't actually say anything.

3. **Hidden architecture** – these are the rules that even you don't know you have until they are broken. Even when they are broken you may not really know what the rule is – just that something has triggered an adverse reaction and it doesn't feel right to you.

Notice when your mammalian brain is operating and challenging the rules or is worried it doesn't know the rules. Perhaps you are someone that has worked hard to be different or maybe you have worked hard to be the same. Notice where your attention is – what happens to listening and curiosity when you are distracted by the need to know the rules?

Perhaps you worry about breaking the rules? I know I did. I thought rules were like the law and you had to follow them. Perhaps you worry about speaking out and saying something that is different to what you have heard so far. That could be your mammalian brain trying to keep you safe.

Many entrepreneurs start their own business because they are sick of the limitations and rules of corporate life and then inadvertently they start playing by the same rules because they are running on autopilot without realising.

Take a moment now and think: What keeps you in your mammalian brain?

What do you need to settle your mammalian brain?

When you have awareness of when you are operating from mammalian or reptilian you can pay attention to patterns and triggers and then develop strategies to stay in your clarity brain more of the time. I explain a bit more about the clarity brain below.

Our hidden architecture is like the engine that drives our actions and our decisions and most of us are not consciously aware of the rules we are playing our life by. By changing the way you listen you are more likely to discover what triggers your reptilian and mammalian brain to kick in and practical ways to settle it. We don't want to lose the strength of the survival brain which kicks in and works on autopilot when we need it, as this is vital for our survival – but we do want to ensure that it only kicks in when there really is a crisis.

Neocortex brain – clarity brain

All the time you are operating, thinking and therefore communicating from the reptilian and mammalian brain it is likely that you won't have words to articulate your thoughts as they are very instinctive and driven by your emotions. I call this communicating from a place of survival. The challenge we have is that when we communicate from there, the brain takes blood from your clarity brain and surges it out to your hands and feet to set you up to be ready to fight or flee. This physically drains your brain of the resources you need to think, learn, process and gain that clarity you are wanting.

If you are not listening to your critic and consistently updating it with the new data and rules you want to play your life by then you may end up here. You are likely to communicate from a place of fear and usually be critical of you, someone else or the situation. This rarely gets you the response you want and when questioned why you are behaving in a particular way you can rarely explain it rationally.

These are very much instinctual and intuitive responses. Even though you might think it is not possible you can slow your thinking down to notice what is happening in the moment. Some of my clients say, "I don't know; it just happens, it is instant." But I when I invite them over time to be curious it is possible to notice what happens just before and what happens in between. And with each iteration and each level of awareness you start to understand your own step by step process.

The questions I used at the beginning of this section were designed to ensure you had asked your brain what it needed to read and learn. And sometimes we don't know what we need until we don't have it. The more you listen and notice, the more you can update your system and resource yourself to stay in, and communicate from, your clarity brain.

When you operate from your clarity brain you can learn and engage with communication from a place of curiosity not fear.

Critic alert

If you are feeling agitated and you cannot instantly put your finger on it then take a moment and listen to your critic. Perhaps right now the curiosity section seems to be going on for ages and you are wondering when I will talk about the next step. That will be down to the way you personally think and the way you process information. It is very likely that a rule of yours has been broken or your survival brain has kicked in.

Perhaps your survival brain is questioning what is happening because the book is not revealing itself in the way you expected or predicted. You will have previous experiences of reading books and your brain will have stored those patterns and based on that information you will be making assumptions and have expectations. That is how all our brains make sense. When it is working for us that is great. When it is not working you might spend more time having a conversation with your critic about what should be happening than you do actually listening and learning.

Now apply that thinking to other areas of your life. In the moment you may not know which rule it is or even that you have a rule, but I can guarantee that there is very likely to be one. By taking time to understand what the rule is and then checking if it is still valid in this current context, you can manage your critic and update your system. You can decide if it is a rule you want to keep or not.

Many of us can have rules passed down through the generations and we can be completely unaware we have that rule or core belief. We may not even agree with the rule and yet we are making decisions based on those thoughts and feelings.

Mark and I discovered we had some bizarre rules around

money and worth. I had a rule that Mark was more important because he earned the money. This impacted how I felt about myself, how I spoke to him about money and it impacted my decision making process when it came to spending money. I had another that without a wage I had no say. Whilst I often had a say I did it with attitude because my system was running with two rules: I am an equal and I don't have a say. When you get really curious it starts to make sense of why you are agitated or irritated by certain things. Then you have a choice to update your system, delete or amend the rule, and disconnect that emotional trigger.

When you feel agitated be curious and pay attention in the moment. What triggered your response?

Is there a rule or belief that is driving that reaction?

It is worth listening to what your critic is saying and really asking questions like: Where does that rule come from?

All too often they are old rules that we just don't believe ourselves and we don't mean to operate from that perspective any more.

What is happening now to curiosity?

5 senses

When you listen you are using all of your senses to process information even if you are not consciously aware of it. Each of us stores and recalls information in our own unique way, and it is likely we have collected some rules that are just not true about how you think we should hear things or how others are better or different. And when you don't seem to be doing things the same as other people or perhaps they are not doing it the same as you it is easy for your critic to make assumptions about what is right or wrong or how you need to be to fit in.

The 5 senses activity which was devised by Caitlin Walker has had a profound impact on my own personal understanding and acceptances of how I hear and process using my different senses. It is an activity that when carried out in a group quickly highlights our differences and breaks down assumptions by encouraging the group to become curious about how they each hear the same instructions differently and how they process differently. With each sense it builds a mutual respect and understanding that we are not being awkward or ignorant; we genuinely don't hear or process the information in the same way as others do.

The activity can give you insights that then make sense of why in the past you have not been able to hear or carry out an instruction. With each iteration you have an opportunity to notice change, update your brain and develop senses that perhaps are not as well developed as others.

I have done this activity many times and it always fascinates me how much I learn about myself. I realise we are not a group and it is just you and I right now. But I hope as I share the activity it will give you some insights and understanding and maybe you might get curious enough to ask some trusted friends and compare your responses.

This is typically done with small groups of 6–12 in a circle. That group might be a team, a peer learning group or even a family.

Then as a group you are given one clear short instruction which invites you to explore each of the 5 senses.

See
Hear
Smell
Taste
Touch

So for example the group may be asked to see a bridge and on another occasion they may be asked to see an elephant. The intention is to explore what happens when asked to 'see' something. Then once they have been given the instruction the group one by one are invited to share what they see. They might be asked questions like "What kind of bridge?" Each person describes what they see. And sometimes we might explore what was the first thing that happened just after you heard the instruction or where is the bridge? Or where is the elephant?

Each person is asked a couple of questions and then the facilitator might ask, "Who has a bridge or elephant that is different to that?"

I am always fascinated to hear the individual sorting processes and how the individual retrieves the information. And given that the group are given quite a bit of time to process this information it also reminds me just how long it takes some of us to process and assimilate our responses. And yet in everyday life you might be aware that you are rarely given much time to think before answering or perhaps you don't give yourself much time to think.

By asking questions and asking the group to be curious about similarities and differences it soon becomes apparent that some use their imagination and simply make it up, and some recall an actual memory which could be a real life experience or a movie. Then there are the differences between the time frames from which the memory is recalled – some recall it from years ago and some from a few minutes ago. What the activity highlights is that the minute someone says "see a bridge or see an elephant" each and every one of us creates our own vision for it and they are never the same.

In one of the groups:

- One person saw a beautiful stone bridge in the Cotswolds over a cool running stream that they saw on their holidays recently. They gestured to their right in the air.
- Another saw the San Francisco bridge which they had seen on a postcard from a family relative many years ago. They both said the image of the bridge was in their head.
- I saw a painting by Monet of lilies and the wooden bridge. I saw the painting on the wall in front of me and I instantly connected this image with my best friend as it is one of her

favourite artists. Only it wasn't actually on the wall. I was just imagining it.

- Another group member saw their bridge in the room just in front of them; it was wooden and they could smell the wood and it was just there and they could almost touch it.
- One person was looking around the room baffled and wondering where the bridges were that we could all see.

The last person had heard the instruction 'see' the bridge and as they heard others describing their bridges they assumed there was an actual bridge to be seen, so they began looking out the window and around the room for an 'actual' bridge and could not find one.

Imagine what it must be like to be in a group and being the only person who cannot see a bridge. Imagine what it is like for someone who doesn't have the capacity to see things that are not physically there. Perhaps you are someone that finds it impossible to visualise things? What is that like for you?

Now imagine what happens to your brain and ability to be curious if others infer you are doing something wrong or that you are stupid for not being able to do such a simple task.

What happens to clarity and confidence?

Notice how often you say, "See what I mean" or "I see what you are saying". I am not inferring that you should change what you say; I am simply inviting you to be aware that some people may not be able to hear and therefore process that instruction and even if they do hear it, they could well see or feel something completely different to you.

This activity continues and with each iteration the group are encouraged to notice patterns and differences.

I remember running this session for the first time and one lady was really quite upset. She thought it was a wind-up. We were using the elephant in the example and so we had asked the group to see an elephant. She thought we had hidden the elephant in the room and that we were not telling her where it was.

I run this at the beginning of a number of my programmes and this same lady attended a number of sessions and each time she did it she would get the same result. Two things happened:

1. She stopped being stressed because she understood how her brain worked and why she couldn't see it.
2. One day she suddenly could see the elephant.

The activity continues and you explore different things and compare responses to instructions like:

- Hear music
- Smell smoke
- Taste lemon
- Touch velvet

Everyone is different and I still cannot hear music or hear an alarm. I can often see the alarm and see the music but I cannot actually hear the thing that I am invited to explore. I have heard people say they have a song stuck in their head and I have never experienced it. Music for me is often a fleeting moment and it has gone. Music just doesn't stay in my head. In fact, most things that I only hear and don't also see and feel also rarely stay with me. Knowing this has meant I can do something about it; I can create visuals and notice my emotions so that I have used some of my other senses when I want to remember information.

My daughter is very musical, and she easily recalls music. This has caused some conflict when she would play her piece of music and then days later I would not be able to recall it. She inferred from this that I was not interested and I inferred I was a bad mother for not remembering. When we learned about how our senses worked we were able to find new ways to communicate and share her love of music. Now we listen to a song in the moment and we discuss it and neither of us gets frustrated because I can't remember a song from last week.

The intention of the 5 senses activity is to break down assumptions and to make people aware that the minute we all speak each of us is creating our own model in our head to gain some kind of clarity. And each of us stores and recalls information in a different way. That is why we need to be more curious and ask more questions.

When we are listening all we can do is make up our own model based on how we hear the information and our past experience and understanding. The more curious you become about your own models the more accurately you can communicate what is happening for you. The more curious you become about how you and others see and hear the same thing the fewer misunderstandings will happen.

If you truly believe there is only one way to hear the same instruction, you can get stuck in your mammalian brain blaming others for not listening or not following the rules or not doing it the right way. When often it is as simple as someone having heard and processed the same information differently.

Once you know how your senses work then you can use it to improve how you manage your critic. For example, some people will always see something first regardless of the sense they are instructed to use. If they are asked to hear an alarm they will see an alarm. When instructed to feel velvet they will see velvet. And so on.

Once you know how your senses work for you then you can proactively tune into and use your predominant sense.

For example, one client who wanted to remember to ask herself the questions put visual reminders around her home. So she had the question "What would you like to have happen?" on her bedroom door and "What is working?" was on her fridge. Whereas another client who was predominantly audio recorded them on her phone and created a playlist that reminded her to ask more questions.

If you are someone who instantly recalls smells perhaps you might choose a smell that you associate with your strengths or the new behaviour or habit you want to create. Every time you smell it, you are reminded of what you want.

If you are someone that feels things then you might have

something you can touch, that you associate with success or happiness or whatever it is that you want to achieve.

What is happening to curiosity now? Are you noticing any changes? Make a note of how long you have been reading and what is happening to your critic.

Questioning skills

As mentioned before, fundamental to curiosity is your ability to ask questions. And I have over the years discovered that not everyone likes asking or answering lots of questions.

I was so thrilled by the difference listening made to me, I rushed out of training and 'did' listening to others. When I started to ask lots of questions, I discovered some people really didn't like being asked questions. Which is why this book is focused on encouraging you to ask yourself the questions. What works for me is to write the question down and then write my answer down. You might prefer to record a video or an audio but don't make the mistake I did and start practising by asking other people the questions rather than asking yourself the questions. By all means give the questions to a friend and get them to ask you the questions. But try to avoid doing this to others before you can manage your own critic. And there may be times like the time with my daughter and my own business where you or your friends are too close to the information and that is when it is worth investing in professional listeners.

Sometimes the only way you can manage your critic is if someone else not involved in the situation asks you questions and listens with you. When you have so much going on in your head it is comforting to talk to someone that can hold the information with you. It is just lovely to no longer feel like you are struggling alone to sort it all out.

When I have a lot on my plate I will talk to Mark or call one of my friends and ask them to listen so that I can get clarity. If the thing I need to talk about involves any of them, then I might employ the help of a professional. That said Mark my husband is pretty darn good at not taking it personally and allowing me time to thrash my thoughts out.

Notice now what rules you might have around questions. Notice when you are comfortable asking or being asked questions and when you are not.

Here are some of the rules or fears my clients have discovered:

- If I ask questions they will accuse me of not listening properly in the first place.
- If I ask questions I will look like I can't remember anything.
- If I ask questions and then I don't understand their response, I might sound foolish.
- People only ask lots of questions because your first answer was wrong.
- People only ask questions to catch you out and test you.

Without the confidence to ask questions it is almost impossible to be curious and manage your critic.

Clean Language

Just after I launched my business I met Marian Way, author of *Clean Approaches for Coaches*, who introduced me to Clean Language. Clean Language is an extreme form of listening. It is made up of carefully structured questions that are stripped as much as possible of assumptions. As a coach I am trained to keep my facial and body gestures to a minimum so that there is no indication of my opinion. The intention is to give someone space and time with their own thoughts without any contamination or influence.

In a world where we have an abundance of wisdom where everyone is telling you what they think you should do or not do, it is often quite rare to be able to speak out loud your thoughts without someone either agreeing or disagreeing.

It was only a few weeks after having gained my distinction in personal performance coaching that I discovered Clean

Language and to be honest I have never really used my personal performance questions or models since because this process is far more effective and efficient.

Clean Language is not like any normal conversation; it is very one sided. It is all about one person asking another person lots of questions and reflecting back to them their words and gestures. With each iteration you are able to drill down and find out more information. The questioner keeps back their opinions and suggestions so that the other person can hear their thoughts and only their own thoughts. Now for the purpose of self-coaching you can gain more insight and understanding by holding back judgement and assumption. Be willing to be curious and with each question you ask yourself you will expand what you already know and step by step you will get to know your own mind and what you think.

During a session if a client asks me a question, I will repeat the question back for them to answer for themselves. The purpose and intention is to empower them to check inside and trust the knowledge and wisdom they have inside before looking to me or others for the answer. You often know so much more than you might at first think. Trust yourself and if you have a question you keep asking others, try asking yourself that very same question.

Clean Language is a questioning technique developed in the 1980s by a clinical psychologist called David Grove. David gave away his knowledge on a generosity framework and I ask that you always mention his name should you refer to Clean Language or use this process in any way as a mark of respect for someone that was so generous and gave his wisdom away freely. Sadly, David passed away just before I discovered the process.

David Grove worked with post-traumatic stress victims from Vietnam. He analysed many, many transcripts of sessions between the patient and the therapist and noticed patterns. He noticed how some questions seemed to empower people and help them to get clear while others seemed to interrupt the healing process.

With this in mind David cleaned up the questions he was using by removing as many assumptions or inferences as possible. I want to give you an example of what I mean when I say David Grove cleaned up the questions.

If you ask the question, "What do you need to do to grow your business?" this question is 'loaded' with the assumption you have to 'do' something whereas you might need to 'be' more confident or 'have' more time.

This question also assumes you want to grow your business, whereas you might want to sell or even simply sustain it. Each assumption means that no matter how your brain processes information it has to filter this first. Your brain has to take time to decide what you need to do and whether you even want to grow the business.

When you are answering questions like this it can take longer and invariably is not an accurate reflection of what you actually think. Clean questions aim to reduce the assumptions that can distract you from investigating what you are thinking.

In this case it might be framed as: When considering your business what would you like to have happen?

A question structured like this leaves the person free to answer from their own map of the world.

Despite cleaning up questions, if you have an overactive mammalian brain your critic may be more focused on what answer you think the questioner is looking for and therefore even with a Clean Language question you might find yourself distracted from answering your first response and instead searching for what you deem to be the right answer.

I strongly encourage you to reassure your critic that the purpose is to learn about what you think and therefore there are no wrong answers.

I highly recommend *Clean Approaches for Coaches* by Marian

Way if you want to know more about the technical side of how to ask Clean Language questions.

The questions

- *Is there anything else about ....?*
- *What kind of ....is that ....?*
- *Where is ....?*
- *Then what happens?*
- *What happens just before?*
- *What would you like to have happen?*
- *How many ....?*
- *If ....were just the way you would like it to be it would be like what?*
- *When ....is at its best ....is like what?*
- *Does............have a size or shape?*

I initially attended training with Clean Learning in 2009 and thanks to the fantastic set-up I felt safe to explore my own thinking without worrying if I was answering the questions correctly or not. My response, whatever it was, was always accepted as how I saw and heard things from my map of the world. I was never corrected or challenged, I was simply asked more questions to gain more clarity. It was the first time I had experienced listening to myself and being given the opportunity to evaluate for myself, does this behaviour or thought work for me or not? I had over the years become so focused on pleasing others and constantly seeking and wanting approval, I had lost the ability to think about what I needed or what I wanted or to even trust my own thoughts.

Clean Language questions definitely make you think on a whole new level which my clients love, and as my friends and family have watched me grow and change I have noticed more and more have become curious about how I do what I do. And that didn't happen overnight.

This process gave me access to an understanding of myself that I had craved since a young child and it is thanks to this process that I was able to map out how I do me and discover that little detective doing her thing.

It is thanks to these questions and my willingness to be uncomfortable long enough to learn that I was able to:

- Manage my critic
- Pull my family back together
- Develop an amazing bond with my husband
- Form successful collaborations
- Grow a successful business
- Overcome my sensitivity to criticism.

It is also the reason I had the strength and the clarity about what needed to happen to get my relationship back on track with my daughter. I realised at some point in the process that the most important thing for her to regain her confidence was for her to know she could depend on me and that my love was not something she could push away no matter how much she tried.

When I focused on how I needed to be and what support I needed to demonstrate unconditional love, my role and my actions became clear. It wasn't easy but it worked. When I changed the focus from constantly asking her questions and turned the spotlight on myself to consider, if I wanted her to be confident, how did I need to be? that made all the difference. When I focused on making her confident invariably I would end up telling her what she could do better which inferred who she is now was not good enough.

These questions are great when the person who is being asked them wants to get to know themselves. Most of the time my daughter would say "Don't ask me those coaching questions" or "Don't coach me". I was needing to understand her but she didn't want to understand herself at that point. And there have been a few times when my children do want greater understanding and then they will come to me and ask me to ask questions.

About a year before I kicked my daughter out these questions were really useful in supporting her through change. She was part of a school band which was made up of year 10s and 11s. As the school year came to an end, it meant the year 11 students would be leaving and the band would be breaking up. She was devastated and quite literally heartbroken to realise her band and her social circle would be changing.

Then one day when she had feelings she could not comprehend she did ask if she could talk to me. I asked, "Is it okay if I ask some questions?" And she said "yes".

With her permission we became curious and I started by asking where she would like to be.

She chose the car and we drove for an hour so. Before I knew about the importance of space I probably would have insisted on staying and made her sit with me where I was comfortable.

When we got back I went off to make tea and suggested she draw or represent what she knew now. She felt stuck and didn't know what I meant so I said just draw whatever comes to mind and trust whatever you draw will give you some kind of insight. I imagine that her critic was still thinking there was a right or wrong way. I reassured her that maybe she didn't know anything new and if she didn't that was okay.

When I came back into the room she had copied the picture of a rose hanging on the wall and a Christian cross. I asked her questions by simply pointing and asking, "Is there anything else about …?"

She said, "It is like a great pool of gloomy death."

As her mum the thought crossed my mind that, oh no, my daughter is depressed, but I knew to keep my assumptions in check.

I asked, "Is there anything else about …?" and gestured to the other item.

She said, "Well that was supposed to be a cross, but it looks more like the Nazi swastika."

Again I was thinking, blimey, she really can only see the doom and gloom, but I resisted trying to move her on and make her feel better and I just held that space for her. As we sat with long periods of quiet, I asked more questions and she explained that the feeling she was feeling was a bit like when my mum had died.

Again pangs of guilt came over me because I knew I had I tried but I was sure I did not do enough to support her with my mum's death. I was just about coping with my own grief and regret. But I had to manage my critic and park that thought to free my mind to just listen. I had to stay curious.

I listened and asked, "What would that feeling like to have happen?"

She didn't know so I invited her to move space and find a space that did know something about it and she crawled under the table and said, "When Nan was here I felt safe."

My critic piped up again and I had to settle it down and remind it that this was not about me. I had to stop making it about how I had failed, and how my mum made her feel safe and I couldn't – that was all assumption and a story I was telling myself.

Instead I asked her to find another space that knew something else about feeling safe and she found a space that knew something about music. She moved to a space in the room near our music collection.

As I listened and managed my critic, I was able to hold back judgement of myself and her and then I asked her if that was a good place to stop.

She said "Yes" and I asked, "What do you know now?"

She said, "I realise I have a choice. I can look at that picture and see a deep gloomy pool of death or I can see a rose. I am sad that my band is splitting up so I am going be sad until Saturday and then I am going to be happy."

That was on Tuesday and it was just as she said – she was sad, angry and all other kinds of emotions and we as a family knew what was happening and we could support her.

And then Saturday she was happy. This is a strategy that she has now used time and time again. She will give herself a period of time to be angry or sad and then move on.

And for those listening to loved ones who are hurting or in pain it is challenging to do this for long periods of times if you don't know how to manage your critic.

We are human and it does impact us and it is so worth learning to manage your critic and listen for longer. Even for a few minutes can make a massive difference. And it all starts with how you listen to yourself and the questions you ask.

Listening to my daughter on this occasion for a couple of hours gave me the information I needed to know how to support her and it gave her a resource she could use time and time again in the future.

How to ask good questions

The most important thing is that you start to ask more questions with the purpose and intention of gaining more clarity and understanding. Your purpose for questioning will directly impact your tone and attitude. I talk some more about intention later on. For now, be mindful that these questions are for the purpose of being curious. It might seem strange to refer to the tone and pace when I am talking about you coaching yourself but I want you to be kind to yourself and notice if you are asking yourself the questions with any contempt or judgement. Perhaps you feel stupid or you are being sarcastic with yourself. The tone you use when asking questions both of yourself and others can and will make a difference to how you hear and therefore respond to the question. Even when you are just asking the question in your head. Have some fun and try recording yourself asking the questions with different tones and attitude. Experiment with different speeds and putting the emphasis on different words. What I do know is that the question comes out lighter when it is delivered with a purpose and intention of being curious and wanting to understand and that it can seem sharp and direct when you are frustrated with yourself or trying to make a point.

I don't know

Sometimes you might think you have asked the wrong question because you can only answer with the response – "I don't know".

I want to just talk a little about this response because so many people worry if their response is "I don't know" – they end up apologising for not knowing or feel embarrassed or foolish.

You might find yourself saying things like "I don't know how to answer this correctly".

Be curious about what kind of 'don't know' is that 'don't know'?

It might be that:

- You really don't know – you have never thought about it and have no experience of it
- Or you don't know yet – perhaps you need more time to reflect
- When talking to someone else it might be that you don't know if you trust them with the thought that you just had – perhaps you don't trust yourself to think like that?
- Or I don't know can be a distraction technique because thinking in that way makes you feel uncomfortable and you need a break

Whatever don't know means to you it is a response and it can give you new insight and information.

If you genuinely don't know then that is information in itself. That is awareness. I have heard clients worrying that they are not being helpful or they sound stupid because they don't know. Be kind to yourself and let thoughts like that go and be curious. At least now you know you don't know. And now you have a choice, you can go and find the answer or not.

I invite you to sit with 'don't know' a little longer and notice, is it an autopilot response? Do you find that the answer emerges and you do know even as little as a few seconds later?

Be aware of your patterns and get curious.

Sometimes it is because of how you process information and you actually need more time to hear the actual question. Sometimes it is to do with how your memory works. Sometimes it is the way you store and retrieve information. And sometimes you just don't know or you don't want to know.

Pay attention and notice what is happening when you are asking or being asked questions and it works for you.

What kind of questions work for you?

Where are you?

What happens just before?

The more you understand what works for you the more resourced you will be to set yourself up for success.

Repetition

Another thing that is not always comfortable and can feel incongruent with normal conversation is the repetition of the same question or lots of questions all at once. When I ask my clients the same question more than a few times some assume they have done something wrong or not answered the earlier question correctly. Please know that there is a lot of evidence that asking the same questions of the same thing 6 or more times can and does produce extra awareness that only a few questions may not have revealed. Be willing to go a little deeper and listen for a little longer. I know once you fall in love with questions you might be tempted to start asking your friends and family more questions too, so be mindful when asking questions of others that 2–3 questions is reasonable in an ordinary conversation but you might want to ask permission for more than that, especially if you are using the Clean Language questions. A combination of asking more than 6 questions and even more so if they are Clean Language questions is likely to take their thinking to a whole new level. Which is fine when coaching yourself but it is polite to ask others before you take their thinking anywhere they were not expecting to go.

When you consider our everyday communication requires questions, listening and feedback, and many of the people I have met so far find it difficult to ask or answer questions, it is not surprising that many of us struggle to communicate with clarity and confidence.

Much of this is to do with the rules you have that drive your beliefs and behaviour and a lack of understanding of how differently we all hear and process questions.

I worked with a solicitor once who was more than happy to ask her clients lots of questions and didn't mind being asked questions on her chosen subject of law, but she discovered that she really didn't feel comfortable with me asking her so many questions. She discovered that she was not comfortable when she did not instantly know the answer. That in itself was learning for her. She realised that she had created a set-up in the office where the team could not ask her questions and she had unknowingly done that to prevent this uncomfortable feeling.

I encourage you to become more and more aware of how you feel about being asked questions. Be willing to ask yourself the same question as many as 6 times and notice what happens.

How do you need to be to ask good questions?

What determines a good a question for you?

How to answer questions with confidence

When we explored "How to ask good questions?" my clients also became curious about what they needed to be confident answering questions. I invite you now to think about what is happening when you are answering questions with confidence.

What works for me is to know the person asking the questions is asking questions:

1. They don't know the answer to
2. They believe I know the answer to e.g. they are not trying to catch me out
3. That fit with my own logic, so the question makes sense to me
4. And is willing to give me time to reflect before answering
5. And is doing so without assumption or inference
6. To support me and with my best intention in mind.

I started to notice those who really wanted everyone to be happy often worried about answering a question incorrectly. They would overthink their response, trying to self-edit and get it right before speaking. And those that were more introverted, and liked to think before they spoke, really didn't like verbalising out loud their thinking process and would apologise for how long it was taking them to answer. The great thing about self-coaching is that many of these barriers are avoided because you are only talking to yourself. But you may have some old rules that prevent you from being honest and open even when talking to yourself.

When answering these questions, trust your first answer and know that the solution can and will emerge from it. Your first answer is not the only answer or your final answer; it is simply your first answer which usually leads to more information so long as you stay curious and ask more questions. It doesn't have to sound right, perfect or even nice; you just have to answer and through the questioning process you will gain clarity and confidence in your own responses. Whatever you hear, see or feel is how you do you, and that is the only answer that is needed at this stage of getting to know yourself. Later when you understand what works for you there may come a time when you want to be curious how your behaviour impacts others but for now this is all about you and you don't have to worry about what other people think.

You will do you in your own unique way and as you get to know yourself better you will have more confidence. We are all different and that is where the value of connection comes in. I spent so many years searching for what made me similar to others because I wanted to feel connected – then I discovered it is also our differences that connect us.

It will be much easier to listen to others without judgement when you have mastered listening to yourself in the same way.

Listening skills

One day, I was complaining that Mark wasn't listening and he asked: "What kind of listening would you like?" I got curious about this and I was surprised to discover I personally have 7 different kinds of listening and that I invariably start talking without defining which one I want. For me each kind of listening has a different purpose and intention and therefore requires you to pay attention to different things. I am sharing with you a strength and solution focused listening skill to help you gain clarity and confidence to manage your critic but there are all kinds of listening and we can accuse others of not listening without really understanding the differences.

As you become curious you might discover you have more than me, so please do come and find me on line and share any new ones you discover. By understanding more about the different kinds of listening skills I hope you will be better able to:

- Listen to yourself
- Ask for the listening you need
- Be adaptable in the kind of listening you offer your team, friends and family.

Here are the 7 kinds of listening I came up with.

7 kinds of listening

The counsellor

"A person trained to give guidance on personal or psychological problems"

My definition of a counsellor is someone you talk to about problems and it is usually relating to your past. Although it could be present tense too. The focus is on needing and wanting to talk about what 'has happened' rather than the future and what you want to have happen. A counsellor is trained to listen to problems and stay present and patient. When you find the courage to admit how you really feel or what has happened it is important that you are then heard without judgement. I often refer to this as downloading; you know that moment when you just have to say what you are thinking but you don't want any interaction or discussion.

Some people need to spend quite a bit of time talking about what is not working. You might have a friend that has gone on and on about what is not working and you might have noticed how difficult it can be to listen for any length of time. You might be that person who is telling the same story over and over again.

Trained listeners are trained to manage their emotions and hold back reactions that may be construed as judgement. They are also less likely to have an emotional response because they are not emotionally attached to or directly impacted by what the client is talking about.

A counsellor knows they are not responsible for how this person feels right now, so they have no guilt. Some counsellors listen to horrific stories of horror and pain which gives the client the opportunity to get those thoughts out of their own head, allowing them to make sense of how they feel now and letting go of any emotions associated with it, such as shame or guilt. Counsellors have supervisors, people they can talk to in order to process in confidence their own emotions after listening to challenging content. I remember a client talking to me once and a friend who told them a secret and then told her not to tell anyone. That is a massive ask of someone if the content directly impacts you too. The irony is that they had a need to talk about it and downloaded on their friend and then said they couldn't tell anyone. Fortunately, that is the benefit of paid listening sessions: you can tell them and it is all confidential and counsellors don't work with anyone where they could have a conflict of interest. Something to be mindful of if you are downloading to family and friends is that counsellors, like many professional listeners, know when a listening session will start and are in control of when they will finish. A counsellor will typically only listen for 1 hour at a time and then they have a break between sessions.

Counsellors also have some control over what they attract and what subjects they want to, and are willing to, listen to. Some specialise in child abuse and rape whilst others might focus on anxiety or stress.

Generally counsellors:
- listen without judgement or suggestion to the problem
- listen in short bursts of about an hour
- have someone that they can talk to about what they heard in confidence.

I know some people come to me because they have run out of people to talk to. They have spoken to everyone they can think of and either they are feeling like no one understands or they are aware it is not fair on the other person; either way they still need to talk about it but now they want the story to change.

I really do admire those that listen to victims of trauma, whether that is a trained listener or friends and family that listen day in and day out. It takes such courage and patience to do that. It is not my thing. I feel the pain physically as they describe it. I can control my emotional reaction for the purpose of the odd session but I couldn't listen to that kind of thing for 40 hours a week.

And yet I know there is massive value in this kind of listening. There is such relief in letting go of a horrible thought and having it land with no repercussions. It is like getting it out of you is all that is needed. Speaking your problem out loud, having it heard and not judged can be all that is needed to gain clarity and some friends are really great at this kind of listening but most in my experience have a time threshold and get frustrated over time.

Part of the challenge I had with my daughter was that I was listening all day to clients and their problems, and I had very little to give to listen every night as well. I was tired and so I would move into problem solving and giving solutions because I didn't want to listen to any more problems. Had I spoken to someone I believe I could have found a more effective way to clear my head after a day of listening.

Just getting it out can make all the difference. My daughter and I now have drama journals where we rant about what is not working. When I reach overwhelm I take myself off to a café and write down all the things that have made me mad or sad or angry. Life isn't fair sometimes and whilst I know it is not nice for others to hear I do need to get it out of me. So the journal can and does work sometimes. And sometimes you just have to say the horrible stuff out loud to get it out of your head. I have a few close friends that I know can handle download. They don't get stressed and don't try to fix it or me. They know that listening alone is all the help I need.

If you are not trained to listen it can feel uncomfortable seeing someone you care about sad or angry. You might find it hard to keep your responses non-judgemental and neutral. You may have an emotional response such as laughing or even crying. You may find it hard not to say something encouraging or even sarcastic to break the awkwardness of the situation.

But there is something magical that happens when you can

speak about a problem and no one tries to solve it for you if that is the kind of listening you need. That moment of respite, that moment of not feeling like you are carrying this problem all alone can be all that is needed to create space for clarity and confidence to shine through.

The coach

"A large comfortable vehicle for long journeys"

A coach is listening and asking questions to move you forward from where you are now to where you want to be and it is very much solution focused. A coach will also track change and improvement and reflect that back. The role of the coach is to keep your attention on your map and consistently review progress. They remember the bigger picture/destination and challenge you to stay focused on that. Whilst you can have a one-off coaching session where someone listens to help you gain clarity or make a decision a coach really is, as the definition suggested, a vehicle for a longer journey. A coach can provide accountability as well as the occasional cheerleading and will listen to support you to make decisions that work for you.

When I launched my business I called myself a mums and daughter relationship coach. I soon found out that lots of people had decided they didn't like coaches and yet when I asked them what they thought a coach was, there were mixed responses from "I don't know", to "They are someone that tells you what you already know". I tried the identity of business coach and many perceived that a business coach would tell you how to run your business.

I need this kind of listening when I am sick of saying the same thing over and over and I want something to change. When you pay for a coach they show up at the agreed time. Just like a coach trip your journey and stops are planned in advance.

Friends and business partners can provide you with coaching and some accountability but they can also be guilty of forgetting to follow up. The commitment isn't always there. The massive benefit of a coach is that they are committed to the agreed time and you don't have to convince them it would be a good idea to sit down and talk about this. Just knowing you have a date in the diary to stop and think can make all the difference.

I have a number of good friends, including my children and my husband, who can ask me great coaching questions to help me gain clarity. But on the whole what tends to happen is I tend to tell different people different parts of the story whereas my paid coach is able to keep a record of the big picture.

The mentor

"An experienced and trusted adviser"

A mentor is someone that listens to what you want and then shares their experience and tells you what worked for them or what they think will work for you. Some people call themselves coaches or counsellors when in fact what they really are is a mentor. They are good at something and you go to them because you want them to tell you how to solve it.

I employed Karen Williams of Librotas as my book mentor and coach because I had been talking about my book for 6 years. I was writing lots but the book never appeared. I was getting embarrassed. At first I got Mark to ask me coaching questions. But I needed more. I needed someone that had confidence in the thing I wanted to achieve. I wanted to be told what to do and what to expect. I wanted to talk to someone that had experienced how I was feeling and could tell me that it was a normal part of the process.

Karen is a mentor and coach. Karen has experience of achieving success growing her business by writing books so she shared what worked for her and then she coached me to find my own way. Our agreed destination was a finished published book that would build my business and her role was to ask questions and provide support that would take me closer and closer to that destination. As I meandered off in my drama and past story she would consistently ask: Is that a book that will build your business? That was my checker: Was I writing a book as download for therapy, or was I writing a book that would build my business? But the difference with her being a mentor too is that I could have a session where I sat and asked her questions when I wanted to know what had worked for her or how to do something that I had no previous experience of.

As a mentor Karen told me her process and as a coach she supported me to apply that learning in a way that worked for me.

The Clean Language facilitator

"Helps clients to discover and develop symbols and metaphors without being influenced by the phrasing of a question"

Clean Language was originally developed as a therapeutic tool, so it is versatile and can be used to explore past trauma and therefore it is used by counsellors. And it is very much solution focused so it can lend itself to coaching too. The facilitator is trained to ask the client what they would like to have happen and then repeat back their words and gestures exactly.

If the client has an outcome of "I want to understand my past more" then that would be the desired outcome that the Clean Language facilitator would explore.

If the client said "I want to grow my business", then the questions would be focused on exploring that as the desired outcome.

Through the power of metaphor, you would be able to update your internal system and you would have clarity about what you would hear, see and/or feel when you achieve that outcome. All of which are using all of your different senses and engaging your brain from many different perspectives, giving you and your critic more information to make informed decisions.

Alongside this the facilitator is also listening out for resources, skills and past experiences in your story that could potentially support you to achieve your desired outcome. I am always surprised when a client is completely unaware and seems to discount past experience that could resource them now.

For example, if the client said "I want to understand my past" and they had mentioned a time when they explored their past and it made it easier, I might ask questions like: "What kind of 'explored' is that explored?" and "What kind of 'easier' is that easier?"

By expanding and drilling down for more information your brain is reminded of the past experience. Not only are you reminding yourself 'how' to do something, you also have evidence that you have done it and you were okay afterwards. This is where confidence has the opportunity to grow.

The intention of Clean Language is to model out and bring clarity around the information you already have and in doing so it brings back into your conscious awareness some behaviours and patterns that have become autopilot. Things you do naturally and find easy are likely to be systems and processes that you now take for granted. Clean Language is great for establishing your sequence and leaving you with clarity about your own process.

And even if you have never experienced something you can use your imagination. You can explore what you think is happening for other people when they are able to achieve the outcome you want.

There is a logic to most things and you will be surprised what you know when you trust yourself and go with your best guess.

So when someone said a coach "just tells you what you already know" technically that is correct. However, if you had been able to retrieve it on your own, you would have done so. In addition to that a Clean Language facilitator will notice if you are motivated or excited by what you are saying and when your mood changes and patterns in your language and gestures, which often reveals information you are not aware of.

Sometimes the information you are looking for is buried away and this process is great at unravelling it. Clean Language is outcome focused and it is flexible to go back or forward depending on how the person needs to process information to gain clarity. It is also great at sequencing and modelling out your very own step by step process of how you do things.

I need this listening skill when I am trying to make sense of my emotions and things that initially cannot be expressed logically.

The delegator

Sometimes you might need someone to listen because you want them to solve the problem for you. Unlike the mentor who tells you how you could solve it, you want the listener to take the instructions and actually do the task. Resulting in you talking and them taking the problem away and physically solving it for you.

You might need to be asked questions in order for them to understand but you definitely don't want questions to help you solve it.

This is often where Mark and I come a cropper. I generally need to download about what is not working, then I might need some questions to encourage me to be more solution focused, and sometimes I need to be reminded to focus on what is working and other times I am talking because I want his help. But I would start talking without actually saying what kind of listening I needed.

The decision maker

Sometimes in order to make a decision you may require the input or opinions of others. Sometimes by asking people that won't be impacted by the decision you can gain new options to consider and simply the process of imagining the decision made differently can instantly tell you that your first decision was right.

And sometimes you need to have the input of someone that will be involved. They however are not always so happy that you ask them what they would do and then you do your own thing anyway. When I need to make a decision that involves Mark, what works for me is if I can share what I am thinking. Then park that and ask Mark what he wants. Then revisit my idea with the new information from Mark and then go back to Mark once he has heard my updated version. It sounds a bit like we are going around in circles but it works.

The key is listening to each updated version and then asking what you would like to have happen now you know the new information.

For example, I remember a few years ago we were talking about our anniversary and what to do. I really wanted to do something but couldn't think of what. He wanted to go for a bike ride. So he asked me what I would like and I wanted time to talk, time to connect and away from the house. He wanted to ride and I didn't want to ride on this occasion. The conclusion was he would ride to the top of a local hill which has a tourist viewpoint and I met him up there in the car with a flask of hot chocolate.

The hardest part of this kind of listening is listening long enough to understand what the other person wants even if you have already heard something you don't agree with. The key to success for me is to believe it is possible for you to both have what you want and somehow that keeps my mind free to listen. Sometimes you can't physically both have what you want at the same time and yet giving all those involved in the decision a chance to speak can help each person check in and understand how important something is to them.

Also be mindful, if you have been mulling an idea or decision over for some time and then you present it to someone else, you need to be willing to give them time to reflect because it can be challenging if not impossible to truly listen and decide at the same time.

This is when you might employ a mediator to listen because they are neutral and not impacted by the decision. Then all parties can state what they want and everyone effectively is free to listen.

This is where I see most challenges when it comes to managing the critic, be it negotiating with clients, your team or your family. It is actually something as a trained listener that I have to practise and when I transferred this skill to my personal relationships it made a massive difference.

Typically, what happens is someone interrupts or overtalks the other. The easiest way to combat that is to give yourself a time that each person will speak for without interruption.

The Strength and Solution Detective

This is the kind of listening I do for my clients.

After years of training to use Clean Language one to one and in groups I was encouraged to pay attention to patterns. Noticing if they are talking in the present tense or the past tense. Noticing if there are certain words that they become more animated about or perhaps their body language changes. Noticing if things repeat and then asking questions to understand how this all works. By reflecting back the information, invariably the client would become aware of their own patterns.

And sometimes I could see and hear things that the client just didn't seem aware of no matter how often I repeated it back. That is when I needed to find a clean way of giving them feedback. Evidence based information that could support them to gain clarity and confidence without inferring what they should or should not do.

This was about putting their attention on things that were happening outside of their awareness. This is not about criticism or praise. It is about facts.

Sometimes we need people to listen to us and observe us with the purpose of collecting evidence that will help us understand ourselves better and will help us understand how others perceive us.

The detective is not listening to make a judgement of whether it is right or wrong. The detective is simply collecting and collating information of what is happening.

The detective is pattern spotting, which is part of the Clean Language training and in my experience not all Clean Language facilitators are fascinated by patterns or have developed the skill to notice them.

Patterns help us understand what happened and predict what might happen and they also give us choice. We can explore those patterns and master those that support our growth and develop strategies for those that don't.

Sometimes we are doing things because that is what we have always done and we don't know why. Sometimes we are criticising a weakness when in fact it is also a strength and we have lost sight of that.

I always think of the story about the lamb roast. A family had always cut the ends of the leg of lamb and one day someone asked, "Why do you do that?" The woman said "I don't know, my mum always did so I have." The next time the lady met her mum she said, "Why do you cut the bone off the leg of lamb?" She said, "I don't know, Grandma always did." They then both asked Grandma and she said, "In those days the ovens were much smaller and it never fitted in the oven so I just cut them off to make it fit."

The detective will be curious about why and will be checking, is this still working for you? The detective is looking for the connection between the patterns, the desired outcome and what is happening now.

When you put your detective hat on you can start to be curious about your own processes.

For the listener this can be more challenging because there is more to track and listen to. For yourself listening for your own patterns, try paying attention to things that repeat more than 3 times. Once it could be a one-off, twice it could be coincidence, but 3 times is very likely to be a pattern.

If it is a pattern get curious when that works for you and when it doesn't and then you can decide if you want to change anything.

The Strength and Solution Detective can adapt from one kind of listening to another and will ask questions to establish what kind of listening you need to set you up for success and will give feedback and be a mentor if it supports you to work at your best and value your story.

The Strength and Solution Detective is flexible and compassionate and able to listen without judgement.

I tend to work with people that are sick of the story they have been telling themselves and they want something to change. They don't want to tell the 'woe is me' story any more.

I am patient and kind and I am clear that our focus and purpose for listening is to find a solution and to celebrate who they are.

I need this kind of listening when I am working on a big project. I need to consistently maintain awareness of the solution I want and my strengths. If I have a lot to think about it helps to have others give me feedback that reinforces and reminds me that I am on track or when I add value.

The Strength and Solution Detective listening is for those that want to align their thinking so that they are communicating with clarity and confidence what they want. Through feedback, Clean Language facilitation one to one and in groups, the detective gives you space and time to ensure you are saying what you mean and mean what you say.

Summary – Curiosity

* **Set yourself up for success** – know what you want and ask for the support you need to make changes.
* **Questions** – ask more questions.
* **Listening skills** – be mindful of what kind of listening works for you and when.

Evaluate your learning

What do you know now as a result of reading the section about curiosity?

What difference does knowing that make? If any?

What is the one thing you will do differently as a result of reading this section? If anything?

Step 2: Language

"Your words and language matter. Pay attention and notice patterns"

You now know about different kinds of listening and the need to ask more questions. You also know what might prevent you from being curious. Assuming you are resourced to stay curious and ready to ask questions, now it is time to explore what you ask questions of.

Words and vocabulary

At first you can simply pick a word or phrase that you are drawn to.

Or you can choose a word you notice yourself repeating. If you listen to recordings of yourself or watch videos you might notice words that include more animation and gesturing or your tone of voice might change. Perhaps there are certain words or phrases where you speak faster or slower. You might notice words you avoid saying out loud or feel wary of saying.

I am invariably working with people who want to define their purpose and do more of what they love so I tend to notice when people's eyes light up or they become more excited and I notice if they lose energy talking about something. Perhaps their body straightens when they talk about something that really matters to them, or they may slump and look away with another word or phrase. Notice patterns and repetition and be curious. These are all signals to invite you to be curious about what is happening and ask more questions.

I would encourage you at first to choose words that sound resourceful and useful to achieve what you want. Focus on words that are more solution focused. Be curious about words that sound like they are describing what you want rather than what you don't want.

Some people get worried about what questions to ask and what to ask a question of.

I reiterate that asking questions and listening with the intention of being curious will always be of value and over time you will become more efficient at spotting the clues and finding evidence of patterns.

Try this activity. Write down the answer to the question:

"What would you like to have happen?"

Then choose a word from your initial answer that you are drawn to find out more about.

You might want to look the word up in the dictionary or ask friends what that word means to them and be curious about similarities and differences.

You might be surprised how often you are using a word and you don't actually know what you mean by it.

I remember for years saying "I just want to be normal." Then in one of my sessions with my coach I was asked what kind of normal. I said, "Like everyone else." I was then asked, "What kind of everyone?" I was also invited to look the word up in the dictionary. I discovered normal is also the mathematical term for average and I realised that I wanted to be above average. So I had been asking for nearly all my life for average, and I had got it, and now I knew what I meant I changed my language.

The more you know about what you are saying the more clarity you will have.

You might have answered something like "I want to be happy and successful."

So you would ask questions of key words in this statement like "What kind of happy?" And "What kind of successful?"

You can even ask questions like: "What kind of 'be' is that 'be' when what you want is to 'be' happy?"

Even words that don't seem that important like 'with' or 'on' or 'in' can give you insights into what you mean by what you are saying and thinking.

Triggers or buttons

Another activity is to notice words or behaviours that cause an emotional reaction. I call these triggers or buttons. You know certain words or behaviour that really irritate you in yourself or others. Write them down, get curious and ask questions.

It could be when something really annoys and equally it could be when it brings immense joy. Pay attention to your reactions, good and bad. When you are really happy and even when you are angry. Notice, what happens just before the trigger?

You might ask questions like:

What kind of angry is that angry?

Where is angry?

Critic alert

I know I said ask questions of words and behaviour that sound resourceful and solution focused. Your critic might think asking questions about angry or anger is not resourceful, and I invite you to be curious: When could anger and angry be resourceful? For some being angry is not resourceful or what they want. But I have worked with clients who had never shown their anger or frustration and they wanted to be able to be angry. That was their solution and that was resourceful.

Body language

Like words, many people make assumptions about body language, and we fail to ask our body what we would like to have happen. I love the book *Successful Business Minds* by Helen

Monaghan, who talks of the meeting of the minds where she asks her body what it would like to have happen.

Be aware of the assumptions you make about body posture and be willing to accept that we are all different. Some think folded arms means defensive and it could be that I am cold or that I am just holding my boobs up. It is actually quite supportive to cross your arms when you are in a training room and sat on hard chairs.

Get curious about your own body posture or postures of others that result in you being distracted or emotional. Notice when you are energised and feeling at your best. Notice what is happening when you are feeling overwhelmed or held back.

It is easy to make as many assumptions about other people's body language as we do language so keep your mind open to lots of different possibilities.

You might be in a training room and you really need to move to stimulate your thinking. Your body is saying "Move" but your mammalian brain is saying that it is rude to move or perhaps your reptilian brain thinks you might miss something really important if you leave now.

Many of our conflicts and misunderstandings are down to the misunderstanding and misinterpretation of language. Get curious and be willing to ask questions to establish shared rules and to reveal any unspoken or hidden rules that may be preventing you from working and learning.

I remember one of my trainers telling a story of how she worked with a corporate team and as they explored how they worked at their best someone in the team commented that their manager had her criticising face on. When they asked questions to gain clarity about what was happening for her she explained that she wasn't criticising; she was processing what had just been said and trying to make sense of it. She had in fact thought it was a great idea and was working out how she could implement it.

Knowing this now means the team don't assume they are being criticised and when this lady recruits new people to the team she can warn them that she has a curious face that others say looks like she is criticising.

Universal qualifiers

"Terms that give general impressions of limitations"

We are all (see I just did it then) ... let me rephrase that. Many of us are guilty of using universal qualifiers such as all, common, every, always, only, and never. When I make statements like you 'never' do anything to help or you are 'always' late, I have noticed this can cause emotional reactions and responses. If you are using these kinds of words in your language, I invite you to ask questions like: "What kind of never is that?" or "What kind of always is that?"

Using these kinds of words can leave little or no room for curiosity. And it definitely causes others to react defensively. I also noticed patterns, that these generalisations often meant I was communicating from the survival brain not the clarity one. Be curious and collect evidence. Personally I am working hard currently to eradicate them from my communication because invariably it just isn't true.

Statements like "No one ever helps me; I am always left to cope on my own" gives your reptilian brain something to worry about. When communicating with yourself it is important to communicate accurate information otherwise your critic will be operating on inaccurate data.

Consistently check out what you truly mean by what you are saying and thinking.

Sometimes these are language patterns and conditioning that you say and think without any real conscious awareness of the limitation that it puts on you and others. It might be a habit and it is worth noticing if you ever get the response you want.

When my daughter said I never listened or I only listen when I am paid, at first I took it be true, then I started to ask myself if that was true. Did I never listen? I noticed that I did listen to her and I started to notice what worked about that listening. Then I could put my detective hat on and provide her with evidence that I had listened and when it had worked. In doing so I moved from survival brain in fight or flight mode and I was able to communicate from a place of clarity and confidence.

She really did feel in the moment that I never listened and together we updated our critics with new information. I updated mine to notice that sometimes I didn't listen in a way that was helpful, and she updated hers to notice when I did listen. Saying I never listen and I only listen when I am paid did trigger a reaction in me and so it was worth exploring.

We actually had a discussion about why it was easier for me to listen when I was paid. I said that I knew:

- in advance when I needed to listen
- and I was pretty sure when it was going to finish
- the client was willing to tell me before we started what kind of listening they wanted
- and generally they were not complaining about me.

Thanks to this my daughter agreed to ask if it was a good time to talk and we agreed that we would set the timer for 2 hours and I could take a break without her accusing me of not caring and losing interest.

Metaphors

David Grove noticed that people often use metaphors to describe their experiences. I also read somewhere that we use metaphor approximately once every six words. When you ask Clean Language questions of your metaphors as though they are real it can allow you to gain clarity and insight into complex matters such as feelings and emotions that are often hard to find words to describe.

Being curious about metaphors I use in my language transformed the way I perceived my critic. For years I had looked at others and wondered how they were able to be so calm and how they were able to hold their composure. I had asked questions of them but never thought to ask questions of myself. When I started to ask questions like "When I am managing criticism at my best that's like what?" I came up with a metaphor of a swan where I looked calm and in control on the outside even if the legs were paddling like mad underneath. Then as I started to develop the process I noticed I wanted to look calm AND feel calm. I then explored what kind of calm? That calm was calm like a millpond.

I also had a metaphor for working at my best. When I am at my best I am like a firework full of energy and enthusiasm and to manage criticism I have to be like a calm millpond.

Knowing this not only gave me a process to learn to change states, it also made sense of why it was challenging at times. When I am like a firework I open my heart and mind and I share all that I have. When I am managing my critic I have to close my senses down slightly and process information one piece at a time.

That is when I started to understand when my sensitivity was a strength and how to manage it when it was preventing me from working at my best with others.

Someone I worked with once had a metaphor for working at her best which was like a cool running stream and she felt like she kept putting my firework out. I was able to reassure her that I valued my firework being kept in check and that it was good to cool it down from time to time. I was also able to tell her that I would say if I felt drowned at any time.

This was a conversation that was so much easier to have because we were using our own metaphors that represented us working at our best.

And when you are listening you might be creating images or experiencing your own interpretation as you make sense of what you hear and see. And you can end up with the completely wrong perception if you don't ask questions to gain clarity.

I wonder, when I talked about my critic on my shoulder earlier, what did you imagine? Perhaps you couldn't see anything?

I don't think I told you that the one on my shoulder is a bit like Jiminy Cricket from Pinocchio, and the one out front and off to the right changes from a hairy black fly-like creature that is walking on two legs to a fun and inviting clown. What did bug-like mean to you? Perhaps you couldn't see anything and if that is the case what did happen for you?

Sometimes my clients feel a bit daft talking about metaphors and some don't see metaphors. I highly recommend you learn to have fun with this and as quickly as possible stop worrying if you sound daft or worrying that you can't do it the same ways as others do.

Metaphor is just one thing to be curious about. Many of my clients gain the powerful insights without them. That is what makes us all so unique.

Bearing in mind the power of metaphor, there is one clean question that does infer and make assumptions which is this one:

Does ....have a shape or size?

This was a question introduced to encourage metaphor.

Critic alert

If you don't think in metaphor, or perhaps you have so many images appear that you don't know which one to choose, then remember to remain curious. There is no right or wrong way. It is simply about being curious about yourself and what works for you.

I have heard a number of people get frustrated when they hear others with metaphor and they can't find one. I have heard people make one up just so they could fit in and be the same as the group.

Reassure your critic that it is okay for you to be different and unique. Encourage your critic to acknowledge the similarities and respect differences. It is okay for you not to do metaphor and if you have a metaphor be willing to explore it.

Summary – Language

- **Words** – check that you are saying what you mean and you mean what you say.
- **Triggers and buttons** – notice patterns if certain words and behaviours trigger you to react.
- **Body language** – take time to listen to your body.
- **Universal qualifiers** – be mindful they can cause your survival brain to kick in.
- **Metaphors** – be curious and ask questions of metaphors you use in your language.

Evaluate your learning

What do you know now about language?

What difference does knowing that make? If any?

What is the one thing you will do differently as a result of reading this section? If anything?

Step 3: Attention

"The quality of your attention determines the quality of your thinking"

Like the senses, we each sort and process information in our unique way. In this section we are going to explore a number of perspectives that I discovered, where if you were biased one way or the other your critic was more likely to be unsettled and clarity and confidence lost. Learning to identify where your attention is naturally and then training yourself to pay attention to other perspectives can in my experience balance your system and support you to manage your critic.

As you work through this section be aware of where your own attention is and start to notice your own patterns. You might have a dominant preference and this is an invitation to explore and give the others' perspectives equal opportunity to be heard and understood.

What's working vs what's not working

Notice if you are someone that responds naturally with what is working or what is not working. Even when I am asked what is working the first answer I want to give is what is not working. I naturally sort by what is missing or what should have happened in my opinion.

A person who sorts by what is working, if asked what they *didn't* like, is more likely to tell you what they liked. When I encouraged my clients to practise giving what is working and what is not working an equal amount of attention e.g. they spoke about them both for the same length of time, I noticed a shift from survival brain to clarity brain.

I encourage you to be patient when others don't answer as you expect – they really are not doing it to annoy you. That is how their brain works. In Part 3 I share a great business development tool that makes it easier to identify some of your natural patterns of behaviour.

If you are someone that generally talks about what is working and you consider yourself a really positive person, experiment with talking about what is not working with equal enthusiasm and be willing to increase your willingness to listen to what is not working from those that sort differently. For those like me who are more focused on what isn't working, train your attention to give what is working equal opportunity and also be curious about how easy you find it to listen to those who talk about their successes.

By developing your ability to give both perspectives equal opportunity you also develop your resilience to have open and honest conversations with those that process information differently. And once you have heard their natural process you can ask them the question to give you and them a more balanced view.

For the purpose of managing your overwhelm, notice your own patterns first and foremost and then notice if you become more tolerant as you develop the ability to have to consider both.

Time

Time is another thing that can cause your survival brain to kick in. Can you think of a time when you were up against a deadline and you were starting to panic that you were running out of time? What happens to your energy and focus? Perhaps as you have got older you might have noticed you think about time differently? And you might be someone that never gets anything done unless you have the pressure of a deadline?

It is also interesting to notice your time related language. Are you more likely to refer to not having enough time or to feel there is plenty of time? Sometimes that is a pattern and habit rather than fact. So telling your brain that you don't have enough time when in fact you do can cause unnecessary stress.

What about your behaviour around time? Are you normally late? Or do you normally arrive early? What is your definition of early or late? What stories or rules do you have around time? Perhaps you think those that are late are disrespectful? Or those that are early have time to waste? Notice what your critic has to say. How does that impact your ability to stay curious and listen? How you feel and perceive time can and does impact your ability to process information, listen and gain clarity. That in turn prevents you from managing your critic and can lead to overwhelm and even crisis. Start to record and keep a record of your most used phrases and words around time such as: "We don't have enough time" or "We have loads of time". Check in and be curious – what happens to your communication? What happens to clarity and confidence? If it is working you don't need to change anything but if you notice it creates a sense of lack or fear you might want to do a reality check. Notice what happens to focus and fear if you make small changes to the phrase and notice what action you would take if you did have all the time in the world. The truth might be that you have limited time and the invitation is to notice what happens to overwhelm when you say you have plenty of time. Changing your language can change the focus and take you out of survival brain and into clarity which can then free you up to make a more informed decision. Just working on the assumption you have all the time in the world can give you the space you need to create a strategy and then you can adjust it with the actual time frame that you have once you have some solutions to consider.

Past, present or future

Be curious about how you see, hear and feel about time: Are

you using words that are past tense more than present tense? Do you mainly talk about the future?

We all have a past, present and future. Take time to give each time frame some thought and notice which you find easier to explore. By giving each time frame your attention you are updating your system with the latest information.

Experiment with questions like: What if the future were just the way you would like it to be?

Or explore what kind of month was last month?

What kind of year was last year?

Or what is happening right now?

Your language will generally have a natural default. Even if you are asked what you would like to have happen, which is future tense. You may answer with what you would have liked to have had happen, which is past tense. If you are asked what is happening now you may answer with what you want to have happen later.

Which tense do you use? Does it accurately reflect the time frame you are referring to?

Which tense do you use most? You might hear yourself say "I am living in the past". I remember one man who felt that he was really negative and always living in the past, who was relieved to discover that he did actually live in the moment and could plan for the future. It was just that his language was often past tense referenced. When we really drilled down he was actually referring to lots of different time frames. When we mapped out how he did time, his timeline was really close together. The way he stored time was very bunched up. This often left him feeling like he didn't have much time and then he lost clarity and confidence when making decisions.

I discovered that even when things changed in my life I would talk about the old state in the present tense not past tense. For example, I caught myself saying "I lack confidence in my ability to write a book" when in fact what would be more accurate would be "I used to lack confidence in my ability to write a book" or "I am now very confident I can write a book".

The more I correct myself, the more settled my critic has become.

With this in mind it is not surprising that some people find traditional goal setting and coaching models difficult to follow. Some people physically cannot visualise beyond the next day. That is not to say you can't develop the skill to do so, but right now in the moment your natural time process may actually limit your ability to project into the future and imagine what it could be like. And it might be that you do not naturally reflect back over time.

Some planning models encourage you to plan for 30 days, 90 days and 5 or even 10 years and some people just cannot perceive time in that way. Do you remember the person who could not see the bridge or the elephant? When they are goal setting their brains just don't 'see' things. The great thing with detective listening is you can model out what is happening for them and start from there and develop it. If they cannot see it then maybe they can feel it or hear it. I have one client that creates playlists to represent her vision and that works for her. I don't always know what she wants but I do know the name of the song and I can refer to that in order to keep her on track.

Even though I know all this stuff I can forget. I was putting together the financial plan for our home and joint business and wanted to know what Mark might need money for over the next 3 months and so I asked him what he would like to have happen in the next 3 months and he just said "I have no idea; I can't see that far ahead".

If I say, "If our life tomorrow could be just the way you would like it to be" he can tell me what he wants. I then get a list of what he wants and then I work out how realistic it is for us to achieve that in the next 90 days because I can see about 18 months ahead. Had I kept it as a future focused question he would have struggled to give me an answer.

The challenge for me being naturally drawn to 18 months is that everything I plan has to take 18 months. I used to struggle with shorter time frames. To keep my critic happy, I think about what I would like to have happen in the next 18 months. When I have clarity about what I want I then explore: What needs to happen for it to be achieved in 12 months or 6 months? But invariably everything I do is achieved over 18 months so generally I don't fight it any more.

How you process time can and does impact how you are heard and understood so investing time to understand how you process time is vital when it comes to managing your critic. When I run VIP days and on the Do, Delegate or Ditch retreat, I spend quite a bit of time exploring time with my clients because the world is becoming a place that is constantly talking about time is money and we are time poor which creates rules and fear that are most likely not true. I love the retreats because they give the attendees a chance to share their time models with each other and there are so many light bulb moments. Not only does it break down the barriers that often result in us criticising each other, it also can provide insight into different ways to perceive and process time.

Being mindful and compassionate that others see and hear time very differently can also improve how you work together.

One lady I worked with who attended the Do, Delegate or Ditch programme had been widowed a few years earlier and she was struggling to plan ahead. As we worked through her time model she remembered shutting her time frames down one by one. As her husband was dying she stopped thinking past one month, then one week, then one day. And after he died because she had not consciously known she had done it she did not know how to consciously stretch it back out.

Over the weekend she went from being able to plan 3 weeks ahead to planning 3 years ahead and in doing so that freed her mind up to be able to make some bigger plans and decisions which included moving house and ending a business partnership that wasn't working for her.

We are constantly processing information, past, present and future, and we are always transitioning from one time frame to another. And yet our language often is not updating fast enough. When you get stuck using language from a particular time frame, I believe this leaves you feeling out of sorts; that then impacts your critic, triggers your survival brain and results in overwhelm. It can also be extremely confusing for those you are communicating with and that can then result in conflict and that adds to the pressure.

I can remember times when I have scared my team by reeling off all that I want to do in the next 18 months but I am talking in the present tense. It sounds to them like I want it done today.

And some people consciously or unconsciously create protection systems that prevent them from going back into the past. This results in them freezing time and can mean they block out vital resources, strengths and large chunks of time which could impact their clarity of thought. Notice if you are someone that doesn't like talking about the past.

There are as many people who don't like talking about the future for fear of jinxing it and everything going wrong. This is just an invitation to be curious and notice what is happening for you; notice your own patterns and behaviours in relation to which tense you use and when.

Your past and your future are part of who you are and you are constantly moving into the future as your past is continuing to be created.

I have noticed a big difference in my own overwhelm if I consciously consider all 3 time frames and what worked for me was to sustain the focus on what was and what has and what could work. I can't always remember the past and so I have had to learn to collect data and date it so that I can review it to develop an understanding of my past. If you don't find a way of noticing all time frames you may be overlooking a way to access many of your strengths and reasons to celebrate change.

Trauma

The brain has a great system for protecting us. If we experience something that hurts us or upsets us the brain can freeze time just before the incident so that we don't have to relive it. In doing so it can also lock away strengths and resources. Sometimes people don't want to go back over the past because they don't want to relive that experience. It is also why they often avoid people like me.

While the brain freezes time just before so you don't have to relive it, it doesn't always remember to update just after and actually remind your brain that you did survive. Despite what some therapists believe, you do not have to relive the trauma to heal it. You can go back to the time frame just after trauma and update your system and remind it that you are okay.

Internally referenced or externally referenced

Some people talk to think and others think to talk.

Notice when you are asked a question; do you talk your answer out loud or do you think and formulate your answer before speaking?

If you normally talk to think, try not instantly speaking out loud and notice what happens. I am someone that talks to think and over the years I have learned to really appreciate the quiet and solitude of processing my thoughts internally. And if I have a big problem to solve I have to use my natural way to process because it is faster and more effective for me.

I take 2–3 days a year where I stay at home and take a silent retreat. It is always amazing how quiet my mind goes when it doesn't think it has to explain everything. It is a great experiment and I highly recommend it for those that talk to think. I do write notes, and it does require some planning and clear communication prior to going silent, but it is so worth the experience of inner peace and calm that I experience. The idea came about because one of my clients who was a singer would rest her vocals for 3 days at a time and having watched a movie where someone attended a silent retreat. So I decided I needed to do the same and so much learning came from it for both myself and my family.

For those that think to talk, have fun and try speaking without thinking and notice what happens. Perhaps try speaking first in a group. Having appreciation of what your natural style is and then experimenting with the different ones will give you insights and learning about yourself and others. Once I understood that I talk out my answer I stopped being hurt and upset when others criticised me for waffling. And I had more empathy for how difficult it was to track all that I said when someone was really trying to listen to 'everything'.

I remember one mums and daughter session where I worked with a mum and her two daughters. The family were experiencing lots of changes; the mum had a new partner, they were planning to move house, the children were changing from junior to senior school, and the mum was worried that she couldn't get her younger daughter to open up and therefore she didn't know how to support her through these changes. Every night the daughter would come home and the minute the mum spoke she burst into floods of tears.

I had worked with the mum for a few weeks so I knew her patterns and her intention and she knew my style. We worked carefully to make sure the daughter didn't think she was coming to see me because she was broken or needed fixing in any way. We talked about how differently everyone communicates and that some people talk to think and others think to talk and we invited her to come and watch and participate if she wanted to.

They were all invited to draw a picture of what they wanted. The mum and older daughter drew their picture and stuck it on the wall and the younger drew hers and stuck it face down so that no one could see what she had drawn. I had intimated she could keep hers a secret.

Then they had post it notes and they were invited to find a space that knew something about their picture. The mum and older daughter articulated their thinking and the younger did the session in silence. She agreed to give me a nod when she knew the answer for herself and she wrote her post it note and turned it over and no one knew what she was thinking or feeling.

By the time the session ended I had no idea what the little girl was thinking and nor did her family members.

I asked them, "What do you know now and what difference does knowing that make?"

The mum said, "I realise I need to listen to both my daughters more."

The older daughter said, "I realise I need to listen to my little sister more."

And the younger daughter said, "If I don't speak no one will hear me."

That session for me sums up the challenge we have in life. We have to be okay to meet each other where we are now. Some talk to think and others think to talk.

Critic alert

At this stage this is just an invitation to notice what works for you and how that impacts your ability to manage your critic. It might be that you get frustrated with yourself because you are not like everyone else or perhaps you get frustrated with people who don't speak up or others that in your opinion talk too much.

Boxes

Another thing the brain can do to manage an overwhelm of information is to put things into boxes and give it a label. What I noticed is that when things were put in boxes, a bit like when you pack things up in the loft, you forget what you know.

So I started to experiment with 3 core areas in my clients' lives and whilst some clients changed the labels because these words didn't work for them, for the purpose of sharing let's say they were:

Work – that could be their business, their job or voluntary work

Home – related to home and immediate family relationships

Personal – related to their personal relationships, extended family, friendships and the relationship they had with themselves, their own health and wellbeing

And you may have more boxes and you may not have any.

The reason I am mentioning this is because some people would pack work away when they left work and in doing so they left some vital skills behind that would be really useful at home and vice versa.

I also saw clients planning for their business and then procrastinating. What we discovered was that they would get in their business box and plan and completely block out family and personal needs.

I had one client who had a potential business deal and he was pretty sure it was the right thing to do. He came to me to understand why he wasn't taking action.

It turned out that if he bought into this business he would

have to tell his partner that the promise he made to buy her a new home would have to wait for another couple of years. He was so focused on finding the solution in the business box that he was only looking there for why he might be doubting the business deal.

The detective in me was curious because he did mention his wife a lot and I knew how much his family meant to him, so I asked, "What happens to family?" Once he realised what the problem really was he explained to his partner and he went ahead with the deal.

I had another client who was struggling to motivate her team and yet she talked about her wonderful relationship with her daughters whom she had been able to motivate. When we modelled how she did that she was able to move that skillset to work.

Another gentleman was a great manager and would listen to his team with great patience and would happily support them to solve their problems. But he was failing to listen with the same patience and tolerance to his wife. That was until he realised it was the same skill he used at work that was now needed at home. Once he was aware he was quickly able to transfer it and apply the same behaviour and mentality at home.

Notice whether your attention is on one area of your life and be willing to ask a question to change your focus. Your brain is geared to keep you safe and if you don't communicate with clarity that you are okay in every area of your life then your survival mechanism might kick in and so will your critic.

Summary – Attention

Give everything equal opportunity and notice where your attention is:

- **What's working vs what's not working** – can you be curious about both?

- **Time: past, present or future** – what needs to happen to be curious about all three?

- **Internally or externally referenced** – be willing to experiment with different styles.

- **Boxes** – take care not to box away the answer you are looking for.

Evaluate your learning

What do you know now about your attention?

What difference does knowing that make, if any?

What is the one thing you will do differently as a result of reading this section? If anything?

Step 4: Reflection

"Sometimes the answers are in your past and sometimes they are right in front of you"

At the heart of Clean Language is the art of reflection. The facilitator's role is to reflect your words, behaviour and patterns back to you, so that you can get to know yourself. This is a form of controlled feedback where you as the client know the facilitator is reflecting back your words exactly to help you gain clarity about yourself.

But there are other reflections. Some are obvious like when a friend or colleague gives you their feedback, opinions or suggestions. And there are those moments when the behaviour or response of others causes a reaction in you. We talked about triggers and buttons before and I believe that when we pay attention to what or who caused those reactions we gain another perspective and I also call these reflections.

And then there is the art of reflecting where you reflect on what just happened and that can be over various time frames. It could be what just happened like the minute before and it could be what happened last year. We have talked a little about different time frames in the Attention section. Sometimes the answers you are looking for are in your past and that can be difficult for those that are naturally drawn to the future or if you don't want to go back over things. Either way, reflection in my experience is a great way to gain clarity if planning forward isn't working. In this section you will be exploring how to develop the skill of reflection.

Mirror-Mirror

When a Clean Language facilitator listens they are quite literally reflecting you back to you so it is a bit like looking in the mirror and really looking closely at yourself. Over the iterations you can and will become aware of your own patterns. You might hear yourself saying things like: "I've been here before" or "This isn't the first time".

Sometimes you are just too close to your own content and behaviour to notice your own patterns. As I share these tools and models with you it is very likely you will notice patterns in those around you much faster than you might notice them in yourself. This section is about how you can use these insights to gain clarity and confidence about yourself.

Imagine for a moment that everything you say or do can be reflected back to you by those around you.

What if the thing that annoys you about others was simply a reflection of a behaviour or traits you had but were not aware of? What if the thing you most admire about someone else was actually an example of your strengths and how you add value?

I became curious about this concept after reading the book *Loving What Is* by Byron Katie, which describes her method of self-inquiry, called The Work.

There was one activity in particular called the 'Judge-Your-Neighbour Worksheet' that struck a chord and really made a difference. It drastically reduced how much I criticised myself and others and it encouraged me to really challenge my thinking if I caught myself being critical, jealous or even in awe of someone else. Using this process, I could turn that awareness around as a reflection and use the insights to develop my understanding of myself and my map of the world. Often without even talking to the person in question. Katie suggests that you write down what frustrates or angers you about the other person. Then you put each statement up against four questions, one of which I particularly like: Is it true?

So if one of your statements is "My partner should listen to me," you ask yourself, "Is that true?" You meditate on that question and wait until you find a yes or a no, without any ands or buts. (If you find yourself justifying or defending, you are not answering the question.) If your answer is "Yes," you ask the second question: "Can you absolutely know that it's true?" The third question is "How do you react, what happens, when you believe that thought?" And the fourth question is "Who would you be without the thought?"

After you meditate on these four questions – this can take hours – you find what Katie calls 'turnarounds,' which are a way of experiencing the opposite of what you believe. For the thought "My partner should listen to me", one turnaround is "My partner shouldn't listen to me." Then you find at least three specific, genuine examples of how that opposite is as true as your original statement, or even truer. Another turnaround is "I should listen to my partner." A third is "I should listen to me."

The more I played with this concept the more I noticed that sometimes I was actually jealous. They had something I thought I couldn't have and I wanted it.

Take the not listening as an example. I was on some occasions jealous they could zone everything and everyone else out and not be impacted by those around them.

I remember the first time Mark and I did this activity; we had a particular person in mind that had pushed our buttons. We both came home complaining about them. Interestingly, I don't do this very often now, complain about people, that is.

We were saying things like: Why do they do that? Is that really necessary?

That night as we lay in bed I was reading Katie's book so I suggested we tried this activity out for a bit of fun because we were convinced that we were nothing like the person we were describing. We were accusing them of being negative and being all about them. We were judging them for bragging about their new car and various other nice things they had recently purchased.

We started to list our complaints and one by one they were as true of us, and we had to admit we would have liked a new car too.

We realised that, there in the privacy of our home, we too were being negative about their negativity. It was like it was okay for us to complain about them being negative but they couldn't complain about the thing they deemed unacceptable. I am not saying every time it is going to be true but I am inviting you to be curious and I am inviting you to look in the mirror if you find your critic criticising others.

The point of the activity is that it gives you choice.

You cannot directly change others but you can choose to be the best you can be. When someone else's behaviour inspires you to check in with yourself then even the most annoying people become a gift. Of course you can choose to continue to criticise others if that is working for you.

I used this activity with my daughter. I remember saying she needed to be more respectful but when I asked myself, did I need to be more respectful to her and did I need to be more respectful to myself, both were true and I could instantly work on being more respectful. That was in my control.

This awareness did not negate the fact that my daughter at the time and by my definition did need to show me more respect, but how was she going to learn if by my own standards I was failing to demonstrate it? And since defining what she and I mean by respect we have achieved a way of respecting each other too.

At first my critic resisted, and yours might too, but have fun and remember to stay curious. This is just another way to gain the feedback you need to manage your critic.

The good news is that you can do this with compliments too. I found this one even harder.

I was more than happy to turn my criticism on myself but it took a while for my critic to realise that if I could see something magical in someone else then maybe, just maybe, that was a reflection of me too.

If I found myself noticing that someone else was kind and calm, I would consider: Is it true, if not truer, that I am also kind and calm to them and/or myself?

I couldn't always find the evidence straight away. Sometimes I would notice it over time and other times I would recruit help. By asking my peer support to tell me if they spotted me being kind or calm I could receive in-the-moment feedback that would make me consciously aware of when it was happening. This process allowed me to become more and more aware of my strengths and of my many good qualities I so often overlooked.

I know many people struggle with this and they just want it to be the other person who has the problem, or they want the other person to be brilliant but they are not. And I encourage you to stay with it and have some fun. If someone pushes your buttons and you find yourself criticising or complimenting them, take a moment and consider: What do you have to learn from this?

Not every example will be life changing but you might be surprised to discover how often it is true.

The more I do this activity the less critical I have become of myself and others because it definitely makes you aware of your judgements, prejudices and hidden rules. I have noticed that I have more time for the people and things I love because I am not wasting time with pointless conversations with my critic.

The story that always makes me smile is the mum who came to me because she was worried about her teen who seemed to have lost the plot. His only aspiration seemed to be to sign up for Jobseeker's Allowance. So the first week we worked together I invited her to write down everything he wasn't doing, or was doing, that told her he was lacking aspiration. Then I asked her to ask herself, is it true if not truer that she did that or should do that?

I received a number of texts that week as the mum became aware that the traits in her son were also traits in her. He was modelling and reflecting back her own behaviour and she was really happy with her life. So where was the worry coming from really?

He was just like her and she was worried he wouldn't amount to much, but this lady was a very successful team leader for a network marketing company and ran her own business that gave her flexibility to travel and be there for her family.

There was one particular thing that bothered this mum: her son wouldn't empty the dishwasher. The dad was more than happy to empty it but both mum and son were not.

I asked my client, what would she like to have happen? She said, "Well, either I start doing the dishwasher or I accept he is like me and that he can survive in life without this skill."

I had another mum I spoke to as a friend recently who was worried about her daughter and the fact she didn't take much pride in her appearance. Then one day the daughter had an interview and she scrubbed up well. The daughter said, "See, Mum, I can do it when I need to, so will you please stop nagging me?"

When we chatted some more it became clear that the mum was worried about what others would think and how they would judge her daughter. So I asked, is it true if not truer you are judging your daughter and you are judging yourself? Just being aware that she was herself the one judging gave her choice. The last I heard the daughter was doing really well and the mum was no longer stressing over what might happen and is celebrating what is happening.

Once you own the criticism and recognise where it shows up in your own thinking then you have choice and you can ask yourself: What would I like to have happen?

Modelling

Sometimes we criticise others because we have forgotten the complexity of the journey we had to develop the skills and abilities we have now. When you find yourself criticising someone else and you find yourself thinking or saying things like "Why are they slow?" or "It is so easy, why don't they…" or "All they have to do is…" then you can either do the reflection activity and check in whether you are guilty of those same qualities or you can take a moment to reflect and model out how you do it.

Modelling, by the way, for me means mapping out how you do something systematically e.g. the step by step process.

I worked with someone that was great at cold calling and reaching the decision makers. He had got really busy and needed cold calling for his own business so he outsourced cold calling. As I recall he had spent several thousands of pounds and the companies he employed were not getting the results he would have expected.

So I spent the day with him as he made cold calls and we modelled out what happened when he was cold calling at his best. He made a call and I listened and asked questions about what had just happened. And what happened before that? And what happened in between…………and ……………?

As we modelled out what just happened, he started to notice just how many of his senses were tuning in to the noise in the background of the office, the language and tone of the receptionist, and the information he had from Companies House or on line. His brain was doing this wonderful thing of knowing who to ask for and how to ask, and each call was very different.

That day he discovered how much knowledge he had created in the last 25 years and how many variables his brain was able to process due to repetition and experience.

He had a system for logging information that would influence what he said and did next time he called. He wasn't expecting to get through to the contact first time; his intention was to collect the clues and the evidence of who he needed to ask for and how he needed to ask in order to be taken seriously. He was meticulous. He had a reputation for being able to get in front of the big decision makers and he was good for a reason. He had a very complex flow chart that had become automatic to him and he was unaware of his knowledge.

That day he realised why the cold callers he had employed could never reach his standard and so he decided for now to delegate different tasks, he put his fees up for the cold calling he did for the big corporates, and he went back to cold calling for his own business. When you know how you do something you can teach it better and you can value your experience. The same happens when you write a book, I have discovered.

Get curious next time you criticise yourself or others. Take time to model out how you do it or get curious. You never know, the stuff you find easy could be of great value to others and you might even have a book you could write. And when you admire how someone works you could ask questions to understand how they do it. The more you do this the more compassion and understanding you will have for yourself and others.

Power of feedback

Sometimes the only way to gain insights about yourself is feedback from others. If your own internal critic is already eating away at your self-confidence it can be difficult to hear and process feedback objectively. Instead you can end up reacting instead of responding.

This is why it is so important to transform your overwhelm into clarity and confidence, giving you space to hear and process effectively the feedback that can make all the difference.

What can happen is that you either ignore the feedback which means you are blocking out information that really could give you greater insight and understanding of yourself or you take on board every piece of feedback and find yourself constantly changing to satisfy everyone and pleasing no one, especially yourself.

Neither are sustainable or conducive to good working relationships.

Constantly changing can result in a loss of your own identity and understanding of your natural way of working. Blocking it out can result in you missing opportunities to grow and develop.

What works for me is to have clarity at all times of what I would like to have happen and to know what works for me. Then I can pay attention to patterns in the feedback. If I get the same kind of feedback from more than one person I start to become more curious.

When you do receive feedback, it is worth asking questions to clarify and gain some understanding of what they actually saw and heard. If someone says you were brilliant or you were lazy those terms alone don't give you actual evidence that is of value and useful. How will you know how to repeat or prevent it? If they said you were brilliant because you stood up and projected your voice well which meant the whole room could hear you, then you can repeat the behaviour. If they say something like "You're lazy when you sit around all day doing nothing" (notice the 'all' from universal qualifiers) even with this statement I might ask for more clarification about what did they actually see and hear that they interpreted as sitting around all day. When did they see it and how long was I actually there? With more information you can gain insight into the behaviour you were displaying and how that is being interpreted.

Motivate, Manage or Mentor is a 3-day retreat where we focus on what you need to be at your best in a group and we explore how to give and receive effective feedback. By now

I would like to think it goes without saying that it is worth asking more questions and asking for more evidence. Criticism is effectively a gift, an invitation to be curious and learn more about yourself. It is another person's perception of you. It is not necessarily fact but the fact that they see and hear you in a certain way can and does give you insights you cannot get any other way. And like some gifts you won't necessarily like it but it is polite to receive it, open it and have a look and then you can choose what you do with it.

In Part 4 I share with you some questions and feedback models that can help you collect more evidence.

Summary – Reflection

- **Mirror-Mirror** – the answer is often inside us and others are simply the reflection of our thinking.
- **Modelling** – we forget what we know.
- **Power of feedback** – criticism can be a gift.

Evaluate your learning

What do you know now about reflection?

What difference does knowing that make? If any?

What is the one thing you will do differently as a result of reading this section? If anything?

Step 5: Intention

"Always communicate from a place of love and good intent"

In this section I want to share with you some stories and models that will help guide you back to curiosity if you find yourself frustrated and agitated. Whilst this book is about managing your inner critic, your critic will often be agitated or concerned by the way others behave or speak. This can create drama and conflict which results in you communicating from a place of frustration rather than fascination and in my experience it rarely gets you what you want. Occasionally for some it can make them feel better but that feeling is usually temporary. At the heart of being human is the need and desire to feel loved and for connection. It is important to learn to challenge the information without chastising yourself or others. Over time I have discovered a few models and tools that helped me understand why I was getting agitated and then gave me choice.

Power of pronouns

When I visited a friend in Colorado in April 2012 she invited us to play a board game and that is when I first became consciously aware of how much confusion pronouns can cause. I thought I was communicating from a place of good intention and yet I was not getting the response I expected.

The point of the game was to generate a conversation. You were each given a card with a subject and were invited to talk about the subject. There were only a few simple rules and one was that you could not use any other pronoun apart from 'I'.

As the evening progressed with wine, if I recall I was pulled up time and time again for saying "We do xyz" or "You know what I mean". That evening transformed my awareness of how often in everyday conversation we/I use a pronoun that can infer that I am talking about someone else.

With this awareness I became curious about pronouns and started asking more questions of myself and others to gain clarity. I would ask clients, "What kind of 'we' is that 'we'?" and sometimes they would say "That we is me", and sometimes they would say "It is myself and my partner" and other times they said "That we is someone else" not including them.

The more I questioned and got curious about the pronouns being used in everyday communication the more I noticed a lack of clarity. I found it hard to listen when the person was using the 'you' pronoun because I thought they were talking about me. I would then be listening trying to make sense of what they were saying about me. When invariably they were actually talking about themselves or someone else. In an attempt to understand my critic would start talking and I would stop listening.

Once I was aware of this I worked hard to ensure that I was using the correct pronouns.

It was interesting to notice how uncomfortable I was changing from 'we' to 'you'. I would say 'we' because it seemed to share the responsibility and share the load but what it didn't communicate is that I was actually referring to 'them' and not 'us'.

I heard clients say things like "We have screwed up" when they meant "You have screwed up", referring to a member of their team. The trouble with using 'we' in this case is the other person may make up their own story and assume it is more about you than them.

When you are listening to your critic it is worth checking the pronouns so that your brain knows clearly who you are referring to. It is also worth noticing, if you get frustrated by what others say, whether it is the pronoun that is causing the confusion.

Try asking a question like "What kind of you?" or "What kind of we?"

When you are the one communicating and not getting the response you want, then be curious about which pronoun you are using. Maybe it is not clear to the recipient who you mean.

I remember one client who did a video testimonial for me. The lady had recently attended the Do, Delegate or Ditch programme, and as we chatted she was talking about how she had tried to delegate a task to her daughter and it had not been done.

There were some ripe bananas on the side as we sat in her kitchen, and she explained how she had said to her daughter on Friday, "'We' have lots of ripe bananas and 'we' need to make a banana cake." It was now Monday and no banana cake. When we reflected on her language, she realised she didn't say "Can you make a banana cake?" which is what she had wanted to have happen. Instead she had said, "We need to make a banana cake." She surmised that the daughter was probably waiting for her to start.

This happens in business all the time.

I found myself with an uncomfortable feeling when I became aware of this and at first it was challenging and it felt direct to say "What I would like to have happen is for you to do ..." but I am noticing as I become more and more confident to talk with clarity about who I am referring to, that I do have fewer misunderstandings and my critic has less to worry about.

The drama triangle

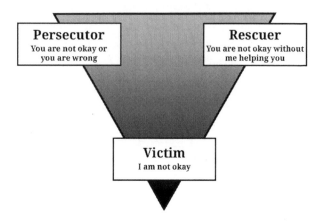

The drama triangle is a psychological and social model of human interaction in transactional analysis (TA) first described by Stephen Karpman in his 1968 article 'Fairy Tales and Script Drama Analysis'.

Understanding of how my ego states influenced my ability to be heard and understood only really came when I experienced this tool live when I attended Northern Taste of Clean with Caitlin Walker. This model made sense of why I wasn't getting the response I wanted from others but also why my own thoughts in my head were neither helpful nor resourceful.

I found I was often in conflict with myself as much as I was with others. I would have a conversation that went something like "Part of me thinks this and part of me thinks another thing".

My mammalian brain didn't know how to please everyone and my reptilian brain just kept panicking I was going to be attacked, which invariably resulted in me being very compliant and then one day out of the blue, and usually only at home, I would explode. I took that frustration out on my loved ones more often than I like to admit. This doesn't happen now as I tend to verbalise the first niggle and get curious sooner.

So the drama triangle is made up of 3 ego states and I would like to thank Sarah Nixon and Caitlin Walker for allowing me to refer to their explanation. I have included a reference to this under Resources if you want to find out more.

Persecutor

This is when you communicate from a place of blame. You will blame or persecute someone else, and from this position you are likely to believe it is the other person that has to change or that they are wrong.

Your detective listening will be great at finding evidence to prove you are right and will only be looking for evidence to support your theory.

You are unlikely to be looking for evidence to understand another perspective.

It is an attitude of "They are not okay" and the problem is external to you.

You are likely to reject any evidence that contradicts your viewpoint.

You could be shouting and angry and you could just as easily be quiet and what is termed passively aggressive.

Your actions infer that the other person is wrong even if you are not stating it as such. Sometimes that is why we don't use the right pronoun because we think we can hide our true feelings by saying 'we'. You think you are not blaming them but you are in your head.

You may be calm or even smiling.

You will be thinking and/or pointing out that someone else is in the wrong.

You will be unlikely to be taking any personal responsibility for change.

You can almost always imagine when you communicate from the position of persecutor you will be wagging a finger at someone telling them off.

You truly believe in the moment that your happiness or success, or the lack of it, is someone else's fault. You will hear yourself saying in your head and maybe out loud things like:

- If they just did ....everything would be okay.
- If they were motivated, we would all be happy and then...
- If they were not so idle, rude, disrespectful then...

Victim

A different drama position is that of victim. From this position you are likely to believe things are out of your control and that you have no choice.

You are likely to look for evidence to prove your point and again, you are likely to ignore any evidence that contradicts your point.

You can be emotional and distraught and you can sound quite assertive. You believe life isn't fair and that you never get what you want or need. And you will believe this is your fate in life and this is how it has always been and it will always be. You have always had a tough life and so that is how it is for you. You truly believe that change is out of your control.

You might hear yourself saying:

- Why does it always happen to me?
- I am always left behind or not as good as everyone else.
- Why don't they appreciate what I do?

Rescuer

Another position on the drama triangle is that of the rescuer. Caring people can often find themselves here. You are likely to believe you have to help. You are likely to look for evidence that proves you have no choice, and that you have to do the things you do because they can't do it for themselves or you can't trust them to do it.

You communicate based on the belief that the other person or people are not okay without your support.

You are likely to sidestep and ignore the clues and evidence that you are part of the problem.

Unknowingly you disempower others, convincing them they need you and telling them they can't do it without you.

You are likely to do things for the persecutors to keep them quiet and appease them but that builds up over time as resentment.

This position is unsustainable and many rescuers reach burnout. I say to people that caring people unlike rescuers love what they do. You love helping and you feel valued and you know the other person wants to be helped.

A good sign when you are rescuing, as opposed to caring, is when you now resent it.

You might hear yourself saying:
- If I don't help they will fail.
- I have to support them; they are family.
- I have to stick up for them or they wouldn't be heard.

Do you recognise your communications with you and your critic being from a place of love and good intent or are you both on the drama triangle?

Can you see or hear where you might be on the drama triangle?

The problem with drama is that we are invariably operating from our survival brain and we rarely communicate with clarity and confidence.

Many businesses are **stuck** in drama right now. The government and many of their policies are stuck in drama where it has to be someone else's fault. Many personal relationships fall apart because they end up in drama and we don't know how to get out of it. When we get stuck with needing to defend our position we shut down our clarity brain and often miss the most obvious solution.

Here is an example of how you might get drama back if you take one of the positions.

If you are operating from the position of persecutor and you tell someone else that they are wrong, and if they sorted their life out your life would be okay, then you are likely to get one of 3 responses back:

1. A persecutor will tell you why you are wrong and that it's your fault their life is not working.
2. A victim will agree and say "I know I never get anything right".
3. A rescuer will say sorry and try to appease the persecutor even though they don't agree that it is all their fault.

If you communicate from a victim position and say "I never get anything right and my life is always hard" you are likely to get:

1. Persecutor – Yes you are right; you need to buck up; it is all your own fault.
2. Rescuer – No it's not, you don't always get it wrong, and they might say or do things to make you feel better.
3. Victim – They might jump in with: "I know, I feel the same".

If you communicate from a rescuer position and say "I have to help them; they can't do it for themselves" you are likely to get:

1. Persecutor – You are too soft, you need to toughen up and let them get on with it.
2. Rescuer – Can I help you in any way?
3. Victim – I know I am always left to do everything else as well.

The first step is to notice when you are in drama with yourself or others.

Be mindful that, like all things, when we train our attention we notice more of it. So be kind to yourself and others. Notice when you are in drama and give equal opportunity to notice when you are not in drama and what is happening when it works. Listen to the TV, the radio, and notice conversations and see if you can identify whether they are communicating from a place of drama or clarity.

Warning

Please don't go up to somebody and tell them they are a victim or they are a persecutor unless you want to be in drama and conflict. These are labels to help you identify behaviour within yourself, to help you own your own communication. If you do believe others are communicating from a place of drama and not clarity remember to check in and ask yourself the reflection questions: Is it true if not truer that you are communicating from a place of drama?

When you take responsibility for your own behaviour, then you have a choice to step out of drama and whilst I cannot guarantee that they will follow I can guarantee that it is your choice whether you stay in drama or get out. How you respond and where you choose to focus your attention can and does have an impact.

Sometimes people are very comfortable with drama. They like the familiarity of it. If they operate from victim, they can most likely predict the response, be it persecutor or rescuer. There is something reassuring about knowing what to expect even if it is not what you want. Even though it is not a resourceful pattern it is a familiar one and the mammalian brain can feel more comfortable with knowing than not knowing.

Read these statements and start to guess where on the drama triangle they might be:

- If they were a good employee, they would make time for follow-up.
- They just want to be paid for nothing.
- They want to have their cake and eat it.

or

- They don't appreciate me.
- They don't have the same pressures as I do.
- I have to come up with all the solutions and ideas; no one else ever contributes.

or

- I have to do it because they won't get round to it.
- I have to do it because they will get stressed otherwise.
- I have to do it because they are not skilled enough yet.

Can you **recognise** the victim, persecutor and rescuer now?

How to get out and stay out of drama

The first thing is to notice and acknowledge when you are in drama. This might be something you can do by noticing your critic's language. That could be your self-talk or it could be when you are talking to someone else. Or you might notice others in drama in which case use the reflection model to check in with yourself, is it true if not truer that you are also in drama with them? Note that you may actually believe that you are not in drama, especially if you are not saying anything and just observing. But even as a silent bystander it is likely you are having some kind of dialogue with yourself so pay attention to your language and intent.

I find it really useful to follow this process to not only get me out of drama but to avoid it in the first place.

1. **Solution focused** – Know what you would like to have happen. Develop your outcome until you can clearly state what you want with clarity and confidence.
2. **Set-up** – Set yourself up for success by asking yourself questions like: How do I need to be?
3. **Strengths** – Create personal development tasks that can support the change you want and increase your awareness

of your own strengths and how they add value whilst being mindful of when those same strengths can be a challenge for others.

4. **Support** – Consider, what kind of support or resources will you need to achieve this?

5. **Evidence based feedback** – Notice, what is working? What is not working? What needs to happen for it to work better?

6. **Celebrate change** – Regularly review change and celebrate progress.

The power of 'and'

When you have all that in hand, and you are now communicating with clarity and confidence and without drama, but you still feel stuck and like you are having a constant conversation with your critic, then check the power of 'and'.

One of the things about Clean Language facilitation is that we are trained to join the content to the question with the word 'and'. When I ask the client what they would like to have happen and they give me a response, I would repeat it back, inserting their language or pointing to their gestures with something like:

And when ....and ....and ....is there anything else about...................?

I would be inserting some of their words and phrases and joining it with an 'and' and then asking a question about one particular word or phrase.

Some clients hear the 'and' and they become curious about what might happen if they were looking at the whole thing, and instead of trying to determine which thing they should do they actually put their attention on what would happen if they had both.

Many people I know work hard for their family often at the expense of spending time with them now and their own health. I wonder how many of you are thinking "I want my family to be happy" and so you assume you have to go without your needs being met for now, to please them.

What if you were to reframe it and say "I would like for my family to be happy and for my needs to be met"?

I had a client once that had three business choices, and wasn't able to decide which one to pursue. This resulted in her not taking action with anything. When she got curious about what would be happening if she did all three she noticed that she could actually have all three. She did that and as soon as she started one became a clear winner; it was growing organically and naturally. And with the increased income and change of focus and clarity she actually had time to contribute to the other causes and business opportunities without resentment. Prior to this thinking she was very much stuck in drama, feeling it wasn't fair and it was difficult.

With the belief that you can't have both you may find yourself in drama. Before long you lose your ability to think with clarity and will find yourself operating from your survival brain.

I love the light bulb moments that happen as my clients realise why they have not been able to achieve what they wanted. Your survival brain is hardwired to keep you safe so it will trigger your critic to have something to say if your outcome is not looking after you as well.

And there are times when you can't have all that you want. Maybe you want a dead relative to still be with you or you wish you hadn't said what you had said. Sometimes it is worth exploring what that would give you, and maybe the essence of what you would gain can be recreated.

I worked with one lady who had lost a close family member and she really missed that connection. She couldn't get 'that' connection back but she could look to make a number of connections that would give her that same sense of feeling supported and cared for.

In the cases where it really is not physically possible it may well be a case of accepting what is and asking yourself: "Given that you can't have what you really want, what would you like to have happen?" There are, however, many situations where it has been assumed you cannot have both or all and that quite simply is not true.

Learn to be curious about what would be happening if you had both or all. On many of our workshops we explore what would be happening when you are working, learning AND living at your best. At first we work out what is happening individually and then we explore what is happening when it is all happening at the same time and something quite magical happens. The individual is always left with clarity and confidence of what really matters and that sets them up for faster, more effective decisions in the future.

Summary – Intention

- **Power of pronouns** – be curious about which pronoun clearly reflects who you are referring to.
- **Drama triangle** – notice if you are in drama and set yourself up for success to get out of it.
- **Power of 'and'** – get curious what would be happening if you could have it all.

Evaluate your learning

What do you know now about your intention?

What difference does knowing that make? If any?

What is the one thing you will do differently as a result of reading this section? If anything?

Step 6: Trust

"A firm belief in the reliability, truth or ability of someone or something"

So much of our communications depend on trust and yet as you can see and hear trust can so easily be lost due to a breakdown in communication. Without trust it is easy for the reptilian and mammalian brain to kick into action, leaving you communicating from a place of fear and then all too often you can find yourself stuck in drama. This section is all about ways you can develop greater trust in yourself and your own thinking and in doing so I have noticed that when we have more compassion for ourselves we have more compassion for others.

Comfortable with uncomfortable

When I trained to be able to facilitate using Clean Language, I was taught to be comfortable with uncomfortable. I have to listen and be okay with not knowing the answer and not knowing where things are going. The content emerges in the moment and I have to work with what is present. It is not my intention to make anything happen but instead to observe what is happening. I am simply modelling and making sense of what is happening, with the client's desired outcome in mind.

There may be times when a client might cry, or have fits of giggles and they may even have a coughing fit and I have to be okay with whatever response they have. Always trusting they have all the resources they need to solve the problem. There is something really empowering about someone else recognising you are enough and you are capable.

So in this section I want you to be comfortable with being

uncomfortable with any responses you might have. Trust yourself. Listen to your body and tune into what it is trying to tell you.

Practise daily being comfortable with uncomfortable as it is a vital skill if you want to be confident to have open and honest conversations with yourself and others. When you are comfortable with uncomfortable you are able to sit with uncomfortable long enough to hear what it has to say. Do you remember the story about my daughter and the whirling pool of death? Had I not sat and listened just a little longer I would have made decisions and taken action that was based on inaccurate data.

Check in with yourself now, how comfortable are you with uncomfortable?

What emotions or behaviour make you uncomfortable? Perhaps you get frustrated when you get angry, or when you cry, or perhaps you find yourself laughing at the most inappropriate moments. These could all be triggered by memories associated with a particular word, phrase or gesture. Those memories or thoughts can be very powerful and are often hard to describe. Being an entrepreneur you will often find yourself in unchartered territory doing things for the first time and so it can be really resourceful to develop the skill of being comfortable with uncomfortable long enough to hear what it has to say.

And when you are really tuned in to your passion the tears might come from pure joy.

You could ask questions like: What kind of tears are those tears? And if you are crying a lot and you are sick of the tears you might ask the tears what they would like to have happen?

Tears can also be a way of identifying another rule or belief that might be holding you back, notice what triggered the tears and then you can start to understand what is happening and what you would like to have happen instead.

In my experience the body will do all kinds of things to get the message out. When you learn to be comfortable with uncomfortable long enough, you can be present and curious and ask that response what it would like to have happen, or what just happened. Then you have choice, and you can embrace it or change it.

Be patient and kind. Communicate with yourself from a place of good intention and avoid labelling yourself as weak or pathetic. They are just emotions wanting to be expressed.

And sometimes you might just have hay fever, a cold or a tickly throat; the responses could be emotional and they could be physical and like language and body language, it is important to stay curious and ask more questions of yourself to gain clarity and understanding.

What needs to happen for you to be comfortable with your own uncomfortable for longer?

Take a moment now and notice when you are uncomfortable; where is uncomfortable?

Does it have a shape or size?

And when uncomfortable, that uncomfortable is like what?

What would uncomfortable like to have happen?

When I am listening to something or someone that makes me feel uncomfortable it starts with a tennis-like ball in my tummy, rumbling and fluttering. If I am really uncomfortable the tennis ball moves from my stomach to my throat. I have learned over time that when I take deep breaths and hold my shoulders back the tennis ball moves down and frees up my airway and keeps my mind clear. Then I am able to focus on what is happening outside rather than on how I feel inside.

During the session whilst I am listening, I will put the thought that triggered that uncomfortable feeling in my metaphorical wicker bin labelled 'Sheryl's stuff'. Then when I have finished listening to that person I get the 'thought' out and I listen to my critic to understand what happened and what I would like to have happen next.

The more I do this, the more rules I ditch that prevent me from being present and willing to listen to those that matter to my success and happiness and the quieter my critic becomes.

Based on the theory (and it is just my theory) that everyone is a reflection and we are all connected, when you change, those around you are impacted. How you communicate change can and will make a difference.

In business I see and hear entrepreneurs stuck, unable to take their business to the next level because it will involve change that might exclude existing clients.

I see and hear families moving home or job and not being consciously aware of the impact it has when their partner or children have to restart with their social circles. The person starting the move is often moving with work and therefore one of their major networks is often moving with them but their family who follow lose their work network, their friends and therefore their support structure.

It is easy to get frustrated with their emotional reactions and I again urge you to develop the skills to listen to your critic for longer than you are normally comfortable with and notice what happens.

Trust your own process

One of the quickest ways to develop trust is to know your own process. When you understand how you work then you can trust yourself and others trust you. You start to notice patterns that you can depend on and you don't have to force it. It just happens because that is how you are hardwired. By understanding your strengths you will be more in tune with why things are happening. One of my patterns is that when I start something I invariably start in the middle of a process and finish with the thing that would have been logical to start with first. So for example when someone asks me a question I might answer with one thing, then another and the last thing I say will usually be the answer.

When I write an email I will write and then when I look back, invariably the last paragraph I have written is what would have been better as the introduction. Knowing this about myself means I can copy and paste and move the paragraph without getting frustrated with myself.

When Karen told me that I had to start with planning and structure for this book I tried but I started with writing, I then did some editing, and then went back to create structure.

That is how I do me. I have tried hard to change it, but now I accept it is who I am and when that pattern shows up, I can smile and move on. Instead of getting frustrated and having lengthy conversations with my critic I can now work with it.

You have your own bespoke process and blueprint. When you model out 3 or more of your own personal models it is easier to identify your core patterns and systems that determine how you work. By comparing the models, you can identify similarities and gain some understanding of your natural flow, giving you insights into what comes easy to you and what doesn't.

You will come to understand certain patterns and behaviour that you can depend on and that is when you start to understand what you can be trusted for.

Take your own advice

Have you ever caught yourself giving someone else advice, then found yourself thinking, "Blimey, I need to do that"?

This is another way of gaining insight into your own natural way. When you really listen to the advice you give others and ask, is it true if not truer that I should do that, it can give you an understanding of yourself. It is really worth mapping out what you are telling others to do and how you think they should do it. There is something quite magical about giving advice because your critic is not trying to protect you or worrying how you will do that. And so your wisdom and knowledge are free to flow.

Notice when you hear yourself say "They should" or "You ought to".

When you give advice to others your brain is not having to pre-empt the consequences of the actions. Your brain is free of fear of how that will impact you or what might happen, and so it is operating from a place of clarity without fear or any rules or protection systems to distort the advice.

It is much easier to tell someone what to do, if you don't have to work out how to emotionally and physically make it happen. The more I explore this the more I realise that my own advice is pretty good and great things happen when I actually take my own advice. Next time you notice yourself giving someone else advice ask yourself these questions:

- How do I need to be to implement my own advice?
- What kind of support do I need to be like that?

Summary – Trust

- **Comfortable with uncomfortable** – change brings about emotion: learn to be comfortable to listen to them all and give them space and time to be heard.
- **Trust your own process** – take time to get to know how you do you and then you can trust yourself and have more confidence.
- **Take your own advice** – if your advice is good enough for others then maybe, just maybe, it is good enough for you too.

Evaluate your learning

What do you know now about your trust?

What difference does knowing that make? If any?

What is the one thing you will do differently as a result of reading this section? If anything?

Step 7: You

"You matter, your story matters"

When it comes to managing your critic it is really important to know and believe that you matter. This section is all about tuning into and hearing the story you are telling yourself and the things that drive and motivate you.

Your why

Your why is like a lighthouse. It guides you, motivates you and keeps you safe when things get rough. Many spend a lifetime searching for their purpose and yet when you stop and really listen the evidence is all there.

Everything you are doing right now, everything you have done and everything you will do has purpose and meaning. You are always having an impact on others and making a difference.

It is 'your' why that drives you.

My why for writing this book was so that my children had the tools and resources they needed to manage their critic if anything happened to me. My other why is because it cost me relationships not knowing this stuff and I wanted to ensure others didn't suffer. And my big why is because I believe that this is my purpose: to change the way the world listens one person at a time. I suffered with being over sensitive to criticism and discovered the power of listening and that gave me freedom to be me.

Everything that I have done and seen has taught me something and brought me to this place.

Your why is in your past story, your present and in your dreams and vision. Listen carefully and tune into what makes your heart sing and what makes you really mad or sad when it is not happening. Why is not a question many find easy to answer so use the other questions to explore your story for the clues.

I truly believe the universal why we are all striving for is to know that we are loved and that we matter. I want you to know that:

You matter.

You add value.

You make a difference.

Read that again and notice if you reject or accept any of those statements. If you have any doubt that you matter, then start to investigate and collect the clues that prove you do.

Your life experiences so far have set you up for success and you are enough. You have everything you need to be great, you are not broken, you do not need fixing. You are love.

Your story without drama or blame

Sometimes in the search of your why you may need to reflect on your life story so far, noticing the patterns and the trends.

Listen to your own story. Notice the things that really brought you joy and the things that broke your heart. Notice the things that really made you angry and then notice the lessons each of those things taught you and how you apply those lessons today. All the clues and the evidence you need are there in your story. Pay attention and notice the connections and your why will emerge.

Try telling your story without blame, resentment or regret and notice what happens. With every iteration you come to value everything that has happened to date and how that has set you on a course to share your message and your story.

When you can tell your story without blame or judgement

you will be heard and understood by your audience, those that you are on this planet to serve.

When you communicate from a place of contempt, drama or blame it is exhausting and it drains your energy and your motivation. Looking back and being thankful for all those ups and downs and for things and people that made you who you are today means that you can tell that story from a place of compassion and education. Learn the lesson and move on.

Notice what worked about those situations. How has that positively influenced the person you are today? How can you channel that pain and that hurt to educate and support others? Without your past just as it was, you would not be who you are today. If you are still angry or disappointed in yourself or someone else, then your story is very likely to be heard from a place of drama and you are not likely to get the response you want.

Learning to tell your story without blame or regret or guilt means you can embrace everything and everyone who played a part to make you the person you are now. Life becomes much simpler and richer when you can open your heart in this way.

The whole of you

If you can't find the answer going back, then try going forward. What worked for me was to model out what it would be like when I am working, learning and living at my best. Imagine what your life would be like if you were doing the kind of work you want to do, with the kind of people you want and in the location you want.

Imagine if you were growing and learning and developing just the way you would like.

Then consider what would be happening if you were living your life just the way you would like. The real magic comes when you pull that all together and imagine that all happening at the same time.

This can guide you to understand who you are and who you are becoming.

Your story has all the clues and so do your dreams. Perhaps you are driven to ensure your children never experience the pain you did or maybe you push yourself really hard to give your children everything you had?

I guarantee your past, your present and your dreams are connected and when you have clarity about them they can be the energy that drives you forward; your story you tell yourself has all the clues to drive you forward. It is your choice if you steer it towards clarity and confidence or contempt and confusion.

How will you tell your story? Who will you tell it to? When will you tell it?

I had a vision of a globe with orange flight paths where I dropped off listening skills parcels and created events that were the catalyst for change worldwide. I saw Mark and I flying together, sharing what has worked for us to live our best life and leaving groups with the tools to create safe to speak listening spaces.

My first why was:

- To be a good working mum.

The more I listened to my detective the more I realised that I had a bigger message to share. My desire to make everyone happy had at one point become my nemesis and now it is the fuel in my fire again.

As I looked back I realised every role I have ever had and loved involved motivating and inspiring others to believe in themselves. When I think about what I love right now, it is that moment when the person realises they are okay just as they are and they are enough.

As you manage your critic the guards and shields you put up to protect yourself come down.

Then your heart can open fully and your head has space to think.

Those light bulb moments that free my clients up to live their best life and those magical moments with family and friends when I laugh until my belly aches are my why.

When I got really stuck with this book I was sat chatting to Helen Monaghan over a glass or two of prosecco and she kept asking me why was I writing the book. And then I remembered that the reason I was writing this book was because a couple of years ago I thought I had cancer and I was terrified I would die and not leave my children with the tools to manage their critic through times of change. I didn't want them to ever lose sight of how they add value and how they matter just because someone was not there to listen and give them evidence based feedback.

Life can be tough and change is difficult at times and yet when you have clarity about what you want and you know your why, it is so much easier to navigate and inspire change.

During those last few weeks of editing and writing I had my children in my mind constantly to drive me to make it happen. I could not fail them. I could not leave them without the support and resources to tell their story from a place of love and without blame.

By changing the way I listen, I learned to truly experience the love that is in this world and to feel loved in a way that I couldn't before. My global why is to ensure that others hear, understand and truly value the difference they make.

My mission is therefore to change the way the world listens one person at a time.

What is your why?

Why are you reading this book?

Why do you want to manage your critic?

Summary – You

- **Your why** – you have a purpose and you have always been on purpose.
- **Your story without drama or blame** – every experience has brought you to where you are now and has a meaning. Your story has value and it is time for you to tell it with confidence.
- **The whole of you** – sometimes clarity of your why is in your past story and sometimes it is in your future dreams.

Evaluate your learning

What do you know now about you?

What difference does knowing that make? If any?

What is the one thing you will do differently as a result of reading this section? If anything?

Part 3:
Confidence

When I first started out as a coach I only worked one to one and yet most of my training had taken place in groups. Over the years I have consistently asked these questions of my clients and myself and with each iteration our minds and hearts were opened to new ways of thinking and being. For many of my clients clarity was all they needed for confidence to grow. As I got busier and I became more confident my diary became full and I started to notice a number of patterns.

Power groups

There were some people who said they could not afford my one to one fees, there were some people who preferred to work in groups, and some of my existing clients had clarity but self-doubt was still creeping in. They were trapped by their mammalian brain thinking it was just them and working one to one with me was not giving them enough evidence to build confidence. I would tell them stories of myself and other clients but they were not convinced; they thought I was just being nice. With this in mind I decided that I needed to start group coaching and I brought a small group of existing and new clients together. I had no idea how to facilitate a group using Clean Language as I had not done my training with Caitlin Walker at the time but I decided to have a go (another example that ignorance is sometimes a good thing).

I had a very simple process:

- I thought about what I wanted
- I asked my clients what they wanted
- We gave each other feedback

After every session – and I still do it today – we reviewed what worked and what didn't and what needed to happen for it to work better. Together we developed a process that worked for us. Ever since I have consistently been able to provide a space where individuals feel safe to speak honestly about how they think and feel, a space where they learn to manage their critic and gain confidence to ask for their needs to be met. With each session they learn how to work at their best with others.

After a few iterations a simple 10 step agenda emerged which spells out the word confidence. This model came about by proactively asking questions that allowed me to co-create with my clients and ensured we were consistently updating our systems with the rules and outcomes we wanted. Neither my client nor I knew what we needed to work at our best in a group together until we started to explore together. My clients named the group clarity sessions *power groups*.

Below is the agenda.

The structure is quite simple and each member of the group is asked questions for 6–7 minutes then left with time to reflect. The group move around the venue, which is usually my home, or I hire home-like venues. They can go lie down, go for a walk or use any space that helps them reflect and think. Then we have a few simple rules:

1. Hold back opinions and suggestions unless specifically asked for.
2. If you become curious during the session, ask questions rather than make statements.
3. If you find yourself wanting to give advice or your critic starts saying 'they ought to' or 'they should' then take a moment to reflect if that advice is something you should be taking too and use that moment to consider your own wisdom.

I have since discovered that this model also works for me when:

- developing new partnerships and collaborations
- networking
- in existing relationships I want to speak up and say when it is not working for me.

In my experience we can all be guilty of giving our opinion before actually asking enough questions to fully understand where the individual or group is right now. By asking questions and following this process I have noticed a dramatic improvement in the group dynamics. I have also noticed that personally I have greater confidence when it comes to asking for my needs to be met.

Power group agenda

1. **Chatting with purpose:** Provides the members of the group with the opportunity to grab a coffee and chat. They are invited to find out something they don't already know about each other and/or share something they are proud of. You can apply this to your everyday conversations with those that matter to your success and happiness. Start to ask questions that encourage more discussions about the things you are proud of and your successes. All too often we only get together to talk about problems and this simple change can make a lot of difference. Don't just wait for birthdays, anniversaries and Christmas to celebrate the people in your life, create the habit of being interested and encouraging the sharing of what is working.

2. **Outcome focused:** Then we set our intentions for the session and I share the purpose and intention of the questions and the group environment. Each member of the group including me is asked the question: "What would you like to have happen?" You can apply this in everyday discussion by proactively talking about what you do want rather than what you don't want. It is very difficult for anyone to support you if you are only telling them what you would like less of or what you want to stop.

3. **Needs met:** This is when we work to set the group up for success by exploring what each person needs to learn and work at their best together. Sometimes you don't know the first time you are asked. In fact, you might not know you need it until you don't have it. With each iteration you learn what you need to work at your best and gain confidence to ask for it and be yourself. I also invite the clients to find a space where they can work and learn at their best and I will ask them where they need me to be. They choose if I stand or sit and the distance between us. They choose if they have the space to themselves and they are encouraged to speak up and ask for their needs to be met. If they need the rest of the group to leave the room I encourage them to experience asking for that need. Many find it hard to see their needs as being equally important as others'. I do reassure them it is only for 6–7 minutes while they are talking which gives them confidence to have a go. The more I observe this the more I notice: if you are taking really good care of yourself and you ask for your needs to be met without the drama it always works. You can apply this principle in everyday life by paying attention to what you need to work and learn with others, noticing when you feel comfortable to ask for it, and noticing what happens if you ask for it from a place of clarity and confidence.

4. **Focus on strengths and what's working:** Then we spend time developing the what's working muscle. Depending on the person's natural time frame they may explore what has worked, or what is working or what would it be like if it were just the way they would like. This section can highlight those that sort by what is not working. I simply listen to what is not working and we problem solve and then later when everyone else is problem solving I will ask them what is working. It is not so much about what order you do it, but it is about giving both what is working and what is not working equal opportunity to be heard. This creates a solid foundation and reminds you and your critic what is already going well.

5. **Interval:** We then take a short break and allow the information to settle. I am always surprised at how many trainers and teachers don't allow enough time for breaks in a desperate attempt to cram the session with more content. For my clients the power group is creating a break away from

everything and everyone they feel responsible for. It is a haven, a special space just for them to take the weight off their shoulders, clear away the fog and leave with greater clarity and confidence. In recent years when managing my own overwhelm I have become particularly fascinated by the power of silence. The more I pay attention to this the more I notice that even a short walk around the block or a trip to the toilet can make the world of difference to my clarity and confidence. Small breaks from asking and learning give you a chance to update your system with the new information. A great way to apply this principle in everyday life is to learn to be okay with silence and give yourself and others time to think.

6. **Develop solutions**: This is when I ask the clients what they would like to have happen and we develop solutions for any outstanding problems. In everyday conversations I believe most people start here and they tend to talk about what is not working rather than what they want to have happen.

7. **Evaluate learning:** This is where I would ask the questions: "What do you know now?" and "What difference does knowing that make? If any?" Sometimes they don't know anything different which in itself you might think was a waste of time. In reality it gave them confidence they were on the right track and it was no longer about making a decision, it was about taking action. By doing this brief evaluation you give your survival brain time to update your system. It is surprising how many changes are happening in the moment and you don't consciously notice it.

8. **Notice and celebrate change:** This is when I check with my clients and ask what has happened to the outcome they wanted. We explore the difference between what was happening for them when they arrived and what is happening now. It is another way to observe change and then I invite them to celebrate that in some way with the group. That celebration might be as simple as a smile or thumbs-up or it could be a Mexican wave. One person asked us to send him a card. So we wrote a card out from the group there and then and we posted it at the end of the session. When you celebrate inside and out it is hard for your system to deny the change. When you consistently update your system with evidence that change is happening something magical happens. How you can apply this in everyday life is to take

time to verbalise, write down and truly embrace the changes that are happening.

9. **Create a plan**: Then I ask the clients: What they would like to have happen in between sessions? I might ask, if they then respond with a long list, what is the first thing that needs to happen. And if they are looking to change a behaviour I might ask, what one thing can you do every day? This is really useful to apply in everyday communication if you have spent some time exploring or discussing something, and then it is worth updating each other and your own system with clarification of the next step.

10. **Engage with feedback:** This is when I ask for feedback and in doing so they are updating their own system with what they need to work and learn in a group. After any group experience, notice: what worked, what didn't and what would need to happen for it to work better? If you can talk to the other group members, then share your thoughts. If not then you could ask yourself, how do you need to be for a group to be like that?

Real life

Group clarity sessions gave my clients a safe to speak space but it was not always reflective of real life. They would leave full of high hopes, say what they wanted and they wouldn't get the response they wanted. People didn't always listen without judgement and they were quick to give opinions and suggestions.

Those that had absolute clarity about what they wanted were rarely held back by this and they would stand up for what they believed in. They could listen to the criticism, feedback or suggestion without judgement and move on without it impacting them. For others it knocked their confidence.

I asked those clients what they would like to have happen and as a direct result of listening to them and modelling what had worked for me two more programmes were developed.

Do, Delegate or Ditch

This programme came about because clients consistently would leave with a decision made and then something stopped them from taking action. The more we explored what was happening, the more we found it was to do with their planning and decision making process. Everything you do or say is impacted by the way you make decisions and the way you process time. Whether you decide to speak up or keep quiet is a decision. Whether you decide to take action or wait is a decision. Whether you decide to eat or not, again is all part of your natural decision making process. And each of our decision making processes relate to how we listen to and process time. The more I explored this with my clients the more curious we became about our similarities and our differences. By bringing a small group together the individuals were able to model out their own decision making and planning process and then compare them with the other members of the group.

This gave them awareness of different ways to make decisions and a choice to update their own model. I remember coming out of one session so blown away by the learning and insights my clients had made that day, that I immediately wanted to understand how Mark and I made decisions. Those models have had a massive impact on our relationship and given us greater understanding of how we can make joint decisions better. Mark makes his decisions very logically based on finance and time. Some might argue that is a gender thing but my evidence says that is not about gender. I on the other hand make mine very emotionally, based on how it makes me feel and how it impacts the people I love. By sharing our models, we have been able to learn from each other and pull on each other's strengths. When I lose sight of logical I can ask Mark what he thinks because I know that is his natural process. After a number of iterations, I co-created with the clients the Do, Delegate or Ditch programme we have today where you can work with me one to one on a VIP day or you can join a 2-day retreat and share the experience with others. The 6 models we develop are:

- **Working at your best** – What is happening when you are in flow and things are easy and you have the most energy?
- **Learning at your best** – What is happening when learning is easy and you enjoy it?
- **Living at your best** – What is happening when you are living your best life? Where are you? Who are you with?
- **Planning at your best** – What is happening when you find planning easy and fun? Where are you? What works for you?
- **How do you make good decisions?** What is the first thing you do and the next thing? What is the process you personally follow?
- **How do you process time?** We explore your natural timeline and which time frames you find easiest and how your natural time frame is impacting decisions and planning.

Motivate, Manage or Mentor

Once the individual had clarity about what they wanted and they had confidence in their planning and decision making process that was often enough. They could confidently explain their decision and often gained the buy-in of others. And for many that was all that was needed. But some found even with this clarity their emotional buttons were being pushed when others criticised or told them they were wrong. Even though they knew what they wanted they were finding overwhelm and self-doubt creeping in when others gave their opinion. Logically they wanted to ask more questions and they wanted to process the feedback objectively but that wasn't happening. They told me they wanted to be calmer and more assertive but every time they tried to speak they got emotional, frustrated, angry or tongue tied.

When I asked them what they would like to have happen and I shared what had worked for me we discovered that they needed to have greater understanding of what they needed to work and live at their best in a group or in a particular relationship and that usually resulted in needing to improve the way they listened, the way they questioned and disconnecting emotional triggers that made them sensitive to criticism. Their critic was still operating on old data and although they knew logically that criticism was part of growth and was simply another person's perception, emotionally they were reacting not responding.

From these discussions Motivate, Manage or Mentor emerged and individuals came together to explore and develop their models for:

- **Working at your best in a group**
- **Learning at your best in a group**
- **Living at your best in a group**
- **Listening at your best**
- **How to ask good questions**
- **How to give and receive feedback that works.**

Change happens when you have clarity about what you want and the confidence to make it happen. And invariably that will involve working in partnership and collaboration with others. When you understand your strengths you can partner with those that think differently to you. To do that you also have to be resilient without being resistant to feedback and criticism.

Wealth Dynamics

In 2015 I came across Wealth Dynamics – actually that is not true, I first heard of it in 2009 at a networking event and decided it was not for me. What a mistake that was!! Then in 2015 I was ready for the lesson and I invested time to find out more. This is a business development tool that made sense of who I needed to partner with in order to take my business to the next level. But it is more than that: it is a movement and a community passionate about the redistribution of wealth that inspires entrepreneurs to create personal wealth by following their purpose and passion. I had passion and purpose in bucket loads but I didn't have traction until I discovered the wealth spectrum and how to move myself and my business through the levels. I was so desperate to feel good that my business became my identity and a representation of my self-worth rather than a vehicle to do good. The report is produced after answering a short questionnaire. It is a detailed report that gives you instant feedback and reminds you of your strengths and how those same strengths can show up as a challenge at times. I love this report because it is strengths focused and comes from a place that everyone is of value and a genius and it is realistic about when you will be criticised for your strengths. You can also work out who you need to work with, and what kind of attributes and skills they need to bring the best out in you. I loved my flow consultant training because my profile gave people instant understanding of my strength and I had people coming up to me quite often saying "I love your supporter energy". I had never in my life spent time in a group where so many people took the time to give me positive affirmation that I mattered. I now pay this forward as often as I can because this for me was the final part of my own puzzle, to know that I mattered. Once you understand your strengths then you understand the two people you need in your system to support you. It made so much sense of why Mark and I on our own were not enough and we needed that third person. It is also made sense of why my business was not making money and I could quickly fix the plumbing and create a business that was profitable.

By working with people who think differently to you, you ensure you have people around you that are naturally curious about different things and therefore ask the questions you would not naturally be drawn to. This report made sense of why all previous collaborations had not worked despite being trained in these communications skills. There is a link in the

Workbooks and Resources section if you are interested in taking the test today.

Summary – Confidence

- **Solution focused** – Know what you would like to have happen. Develop your outcome until you can clearly state what you want with clarity and confidence.
- **Needs met –** Set yourself up for success by asking yourself questions like: How do you need to be? Take responsibility for your own behaviour and how that impacts your performance and the response you get.
- **Focus on strengths** – Develop your what's working muscle daily and ensure that you always pay attention and notice your strengths whilst being mindful that those same strengths can be a challenge at times.
- **Support** – Consider what kind of support or resources will you need and how to ask for help and get it. Find people that think differently to you to support you and bring you back into balance. The kind of thinking you find hard they will find easy and together you can achieve more than alone.
- **Feedback** – Take time regularly to consider: What is working? What is not working? What needs to happen for it to work better? You might at first do it hourly or daily. You might find that too intense so try weekly or monthly or even quarterly. It is not so much about how often and more about consistently scheduling time to notice and rebalance your system.
- **Celebrate change** – As part of your review you will notice change and I really cannot emphasise enough the importance of celebrating it. Even if the change is not what you wanted – the fact you are reviewing it now means you are aware right now and can choose to do something about it and that in itself is a change worthy of celebration.

Evaluate your learning

What do you know now about you?

What difference does knowing that make? If any?

What is the one thing you will do differently as a result of reading this section? If anything?

Conclusion

Letter to my children

Dear Paige and Liam

As you grew inside me, my body changed and when you arrived my whole world changed in so many ways. Since that day every cell in your body and mine has been constantly changing and growing.

Life and nature works in cycles and everything is iterative and the one thing that is constant is change itself. The planet we live on is constantly moving so even when you stand as still as you can you are actually moving. The weather changes. Relationships change. Goals and aspirations change. And as you know better, you do better. Sometimes even when you know better you might find yourself doing the old behaviour and wondering why.

Sometimes your critic can have so much to say.

That critic could be in your head or perhaps on your shoulder and it could be family, friends or people at work.

For too many years I was also your critic. I worried you would not fit in, that there was not enough and that you would not be good enough. That was until I changed the way I listened and realised you have always been enough and there is enough.

When I changed my focus, something magical happened.

I discovered you were okay and you had always been okay.

Listening is one of the most important skills in life to develop and yet few do take the time to develop it. And listening can be a hard thing to sustain. If you ever find yourself without the right people around you to talk to, then please know that it is okay to pay for someone who is trained to listen to you. I know society thinks this is a sign of weakness and I want you to know it is not. The best leaders have confidants and people to confide in.

Don't do what I did and wait for a crisis before you ask for help. Peer support made up of different people who can do all kinds of different listening is something we all need and deserve through times of change.

I know I can trust you to pay it forward, as you have done so much already. You are both great mentors and coaches to so many of your friends. At times it is hard to listen with love in your heart and without judgement. You might find yourself tired, exhausted and with no sense of logic left. And at times like this you might find your thinking becomes consumed by the voice of your critic.

It is my hope the lessons shared in this book will resource you to know what you need to achieve clarity and confidence again through whatever change life throws your way.

If you find yourself criticising yourself or others, be kind and forgive yourself. Celebrate the fact that you have noticed it and then take action and listen. The process of being heard is often all that is needed to put things back into perspective.

Collect evidence daily of the value you add and be aware of the rules that you are living your life by and ditch any that prevent you from showing up as the best version of you that you can be.

Then notice change and celebrate it as often as you can, as this can reassure your critic that change is not something to be feared but something to be embraced. And when you experience change that is painful, be willing to grieve and allow those emotions time and space to be heard too.

Paige and Liam, you are both great listeners and I am so proud of the people you have already supported in your young lives. And I want you to know the world needs listeners like you and sometimes there are just not enough listeners for everyone to be heard.

As long as I am alive I will do my best to be your very own strength and solution detective and I trust this book will act as a reminder of how to listen to yourself if I am all listened out.

Love Mum xxx

To my younger self aged 9

Dear Sheryl

When the doctor tells your mother that they will know when you are 15 if you are normal, please know that normal is the mathematical term for average and you don't really want to be normal. Don't strive for normal – strive for authentic.

Listen to yourself and tune into your own body and mind and truly get to know what you want and what works for you. Be confident enough to be different and compassionate enough to conform.

You are kind and generous and sensitive which means you will feel things that others don't and some might tell you that your tears are a sign of weakness. I want you to know that your tears are a sign that you need to take time to listen inside and out. You hear things others miss and you feel things others don't and this is your strength.

You are strong and athletic which means you will be seen by some as solid and they might even refer to your legs as tree trunks but this doesn't mean that you are not elegant and beautiful all at the same time. If you feel hurt or offended, ask questions to understand what they mean, and always know that you matter.

Regarding school and exams, they are the foundation for

life. They are intended to raise awareness of what has been and what can be but they can never tell you what you are. Only you can determine that by listening to yourself and making your own choices.

Beautiful, kind and generous Sheryl, always give yourself time to think, breathe and reflect when you feel criticised or you find yourself criticising – remember inside all of us is a detective waiting to be born that collects the evidence and allows us to notice patterns.

Remember that you also have a little cheerleader inside you and that cheerleader always believes in you.

And even when you are all alone and you believe no one can help, I want you to know that you are never alone – I am always with you – I am your strength and solution detective. I will always find your strengths and I will always help you understand your next best step and we will always celebrate change no matter how small.

The whole world is struggling to be heard and understood, and you are the difference the world is waiting for. You can start today by listening to and managing your critic.

Sheryl, aged 48 (older and wiser)

Letter to you, the reader

Dear Reader

At this moment in time as you conclude the reading of this book I want you to know that you matter. You are of value and you make a difference. If you find your critic having anything to say or simply trying to ignore those words – perhaps you find yourself trying to gloss over them – then stop right now and say them out loud. Write them down and know you matter. You truly do.

Listen very carefully. Maybe the way you process information is more visual and when people say things that are nice you don't 'really' hear them. Maybe you are more audio and if people show you their appreciation but don't say it you don't notice it. Maybe you feel everything and it is hard to filter out the pain to experience the joy.

Whatever the reason or wherever you are starting from, today is the day to start developing your very own strength and solution detective.

And if, like me, you find no matter how much you acknowledge it personally it doesn't really sink in until you have heard it externally too, then collaborate with like-minded and caring people and ask for the feedback you need to grow. Ask others to notice when you add value and make a difference. Take time daily to record what is working inside and out.

And then when you have an equal balance of what is working and what is not working, invest the same amount of time in determining what needs to happen for it to work better.

Your wealth, your health and your happiness depend on your ability to manage your critic. How can you do that if you don't stop criticising yourself?

Please do more of what you love and ditch the critic that says you can't.

Sheryl

Your Strength and Solution Detective xx

Part 4 – Workbooks

This is the section where you can take time to listen to your critic and step by step gain clarity and confidence in your next best step.

Starting point

Take time to write down what is happening now. What is not working? What do you hear and see that tells you something has to change? By recording your starting point, you will give yourself the opportunity to notice and celebrate change later.

Solution focused

What would you like to have happen?

You can start by using this space to draw or represent what you would like to have happen or for a more detailed workbook designed to set you up for success you can request a copy of the Clarity Confidence & Change Workbook which also includes 7 short video tutorials straight to your inbox one a day for a week. http://www.manageyourcritic.com/CCCworkbook

Setting you up for success

How do you need to be? Think about the outcome you want. What kind of you is that you that makes that happen?

Strengths

Commit to notice and record, what is happening when you are working at your best? Notice when you are making a difference and what your strengths are. Ask friends and families to give you feedback on how you add value. Alternatively, you can gain access to your own Wealth Dynamics report here: www.manageyourcritic.com/wealthdynamics

Support

What kind of support or resources will you need to achieve this? Record it here.

Evidence based feedback

Schedule appointments with yourself to give yourself evidence based feedback. I love the Clean Feedback models developed by Training Attention. www.trainingattention.co.uk

Clean Feedback

What is working?

Collect the evidence. What do you hear and see that tells you it is working?

What is not working?

Collect the evidence. What do you hear and see that tells you it is not working?

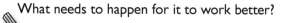

What needs to happen for it to work better?

Drama-free feedback

When you find yourself in drama it is important to separate the fact from the assumptions and the Clean Feedback model is superb for that.

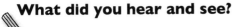

What did you hear and see?

What do you infer from that? How did you make sense of what you heard and saw?

What is the story you made up to make sense of what you heard and saw? For example, when I see someone sitting around I might infer from that that they are lazy. It is not a fact – lazy is the inference and the story I am making up to make sense of what I have seen and heard.

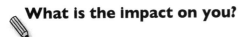

What is the impact on you?

What would you like to have happen?

Celebrate change

Make a conscious effort to notice change and take time to celebrate it and acknowledge it as often as possible. Use this space to record changes that happen and how you celebrated.

What changed?	How did I celebrate that change?

Part 5 – Resources

Books I have referred to

Marian Way, *Clean Approaches for Coaches*
Byron Katie, *Loving What Is*
Caitlin Walker, *From Contempt to Curiosity*
Eric Jensen, *Brain-Based Learning: The New Paradigm of Teaching*
Stephen Karpman, 'Fairy Tales and Script Drama Analysis',
available at http://www.karpmandramatriangle.com/pdf/
DramaTriangle.pdf
Helen Monaghan, *Successful Business Minds*

Other resources

Clean question cards can be found at https://cleanlearning.
co.uk/products/detail/clean-in-a-box-1
Clean Learning Courses https://cleanlearning.co.uk/events
The following can be found in *From Contempt to Curiosity –
creating the conditions for groups to collaborate*
Clean Feedback page 33
Five Senses Exercise page 63–64
Drama to Karma page 129

Contact Sheryl

Find out more about Sheryl and her work at:
www.stepbysteplistening.com

Email Sheryl at
Sheryl@stepbysteplistening.com

Social Media

You can also follow Sheryl via social media:

Facebook - www.facebook.com/stepbysteplistening
Twitter - www.twitter.com/sbslistening

Join Sheryl and other readers online to discuss
and celebrate change:

Facebook Public Group - Manage Your Critic
- From Overwhelm to Clarity in 7 Steps -
https://www.facebook.com/groups/manageyourcritic/